SHIFT & SWITCH

NEW CANADIAN POETRY

SHIFT & SWITCH

NEW CANADIAN POETRY

EDITED BY DEREK BEAULIEU,
JASON CHRISTIE &
ANGELA RAWLINGS

THE MERCURY PRESS

The publisher gratefully acknowledges the financial assistance of the Canada Council for the Arts, the Ontario Arts Council, the Ontario Book Publishing Tax Credit Program, and the Ontario Media Development Corporation. The publisher further acknowledges the financial support of the Government of Canada through the Department of Canadian Heritage's Book Publishing Industry Development Program (BPIDP) for our publishing activities.

Acquisitions and series editor: Beverley Daurio
Cover design: Beverley Daurio & Angela Rawlings
Cover art: Brendan Fernandes
Composition and page design: Beverley Daurio & Angela Rawlings

Printed and bound in Canada
Printed on acid-free paper

2 3 4 5 09 08 07 06

Library and Archives Canada Cataloguing in Publication

Shift & switch : new Canadian poetry / edited by Derek Beaulieu, Jason Christie, Angela Rawlings.

ISBN 1-55128-116-3

1. Experimental poetry, Canadian (English). 2. Canadian poetry (English)—20th century. 3. Canadian poetry (English)—21st century. I. Beaulieu, D. A. (Derek Alexander), 1973- II. Christie, Jason, 1977- III. Rawlings, Angela, 1978- IV. Title: Shift and switch.

PS8293.1.S55 2005 C811'.5408011 C2005-905295-3

The Mercury Press
Box 672, Station P,
Toronto, Ontario Canada M5S 2Y4
www.themercurypress.ca

CONTENTS

INTRODUCTIONS BY THE EDITORS 7

DEREK BEAULIEU 14
pitt graphit 4
variance (august)
for Brian

GREGORY BETTS 17
excerpt from *If Language*
Love

ALICE BURDICK 22
The meat leaves, slowly
Where are our tiger teeth?

JASON CHRISTIE 24
excerpt from *The Robot Suites*

MICHAEL DEBEYER 29
The Frictionless Room
The Penultimate Ice Works
The Party
Light as Air

CHRIS FICKLING 33
Botticelli: Birth of Venus
Van Gogh: Starry Night
Dali: Persistence
Escher: Drawing Hands

JON PAUL FIORENTINO 37
excerpt from *The Theory of the Loser Class*
Binary Code Sonnet 1.0

RYAN FITZPATRICK 39
A Life Less Originary
Why I Like Big Butts

JAY GAMBLE 41
excerpt from *Bound*
excerpt from *Gagged*

SHARON HARRIS 46
excerpt from *Fun with 'Pataphysics*
6x9

JILL HARTMAN 49
excerpt from *Another Word for Pirate Treasure, or, The Booty*

JAMIE HILDER 56
Highway 17, June 7th, 2002
Highway 1, May 23rd, 2002
Nordel Way, July 1st, 2002
Highway 17, September 6th, 1999

GEOFFREY HLIBCHUK 60
Trigonometric algorithm over horizon, Kansas 1953
Asynchronous Motor

MATTHEW HOLLETT 62
rabbit-track alphabet
soliloquies: language
soliloquies: flood
answers (found poems)
speechballoon #0217

JESSE HUISKEN 67
excerpt from *Objectives*

KEDRICK JAMES 69
excerpt from *Abecedary*

REG JOHANSON 71
excerpt from *Chips*

FRANCES KRUK 75
with illustrations by anna mandelkau
excerpt from *The Thought Process*

LARISSA LAI 82
excerpt from *Rachel*

JASON LE HEUP 85
excerpt from *Indefinite Sweat*

GLEN LOWRY 89
blue green forest — remnants
XVII

DANIELLE MAVEAL 96
flowers, fire, wind, fish
black

JEREMY MCLEOD 98
Writing Art Systems Ten
would the remote province

MAX MIDDLE 100
dear jc
2 visual poems

GUSTAVE MORIN 103
ACK
index
derail
voice
going nova

JANET NEIGH 108
excerpt from *The Wiring of Bella O*

A.RAWLINGS 115
excerpt from *Wide slumber for lepidopterists*
love poem for a sailor
cardiology
our tongued jigsaws aphasiatic

ROB READ 120
excerpt from *Hieroglyphs*
Daily treated spam: Amazing
Daily treated spam: ruffian clocks defined by 85
Daily treated spam: The solution is easy

JORDAN SCOTT 127
excerpt from *blert*

NATALIE SIMPSON 134
excerpt from *Tide*
Vallarta
excerpt from *CHUMP*
Notes

TREVOR SPELLER 141
untitled
famous people./
Magnolia acuminata

NATHALIE STEPHENS 145
The Scarceness of the Body Architecture's Scorn

ANDREA STRUDENSKY 147
4 poems

HUGH THOMAS 151
Welcome
Tamari lattice
Girls who eat flowers and fail their IQ tests

MARK TRUSCOTT 155
Surface
Thing
Ontology
Lines
Winter

DOUGLAS WEBSTER 160
02109
one = 1

JONATHON WILCKE 162
excerpt from *Dupe!*

JULIA WILLIAMS 169
excerpt from *My Family Is a Genius*

RITA WONG 175
fester
value chain

SUZANNE ZELAZO 177
Cataract
Infusoria
Vaga Luna

RACHEL ZOLF 182
excerpt from *Human Resources*

CONTRIBUTOR BIOS 185

ACKNOWLEDGEMENTS 191

INTRODUCTION, DEREK BEAULIEU

a shift, a switch

Poetry is aversion of conformity.
— Charles Bernstein, "State of the Art"

Shift & Switch: New Canadian Poetry gathers 41 contemporary poets who are actively working to define poetics & poetic community, beyond the scope of the "expected."

For too long and for far too often, Canadian poetry anthologies have presented a neo-conservative poetic as the "cutting edge" in Canadian poetry, marginalizing voices that work to challenge the reading & writing status quo. The poem as finely wrought epiphanic moment of personal reflection (the poetry norm) underlines mass-culture & political sameness; it does little to question or confront how language itself defines the limitations of expression — both personal & critical.

Anthologies that emphasize the classical & humanist definitions of poetry without considering work being done in alternative forms do little to further the writing of Canadian poetry as they offer only what is most palatable to the most conservative of audiences.

An alternative must be offered.

The writers in *Shift & Switch* actively engage with social constructions, economic exchanges, & geo-political definitions. For Bernstein, poetics is "an invasion of the poetic into other realms: overflowing the bounds of genre, spilling into talk, essays, politics, philosophy [...] a sort of applied poetic." The writers in *Shift & Switch* use poetry — in their writing and in their communities — as an interrogative form across genre to confront the unchallenged: "Make sense; make / densely overpopulated. State sentence; / state legislature" (fitzpatrick 39).

The accommodationist "official verse culture" of personal confession & reflection has been flattened into a sameness of subject, form, & structure. In striving for universality it instead degenerates into an implicit support of sloganeering, advertising, & suburban consumerism; "cartons of cigarettes waiting for lungs to reside in" (wong 176). Neo-conservative writing continuously underlines the relationship between power & language. To resist & undermine this commodification, poetry must become a "granitic, endemic loss" (Betts 19). The poets in this collection protest that "this writing puts a crimp in my throat, back deep resounding" (Simpson 135) — a tightening of the vocal (& written) chords when faced with the impossibility of speaking when, as Steve McCaffery stated, "language [...] functions like money and speaks through us more than we actively produce within it."

The poets in *Shift & Switch* construct writing that is actively aware of its own economic & rhetorical position. If "the language we use / is the language we desire" (Hartman 50), these writers yearn for a language stretching beyond the normal into a poetry of the margin. Poetic language becomes a category that includes found text, mathematics, prose forms, photography, performance & concrete poetry, all of which are beyond the traditional definitions of poetry that are commonly accepted. The poets in *Shift & Switch* eschew & disrupt "normal" language; instead they — as Janet Neigh writes — "absorb" their "own beating speech without echoing back" (112) the narrative of closure & consumption.

The poets in *Shift & Switch: New Canadian Poetry* are consciously attempting to resist & interrogate conformity — to push not only against the friction of categorization, but against language's own limitations. These are voices that cleave a space, by seizing language itself, manipulating it in a way that offers new alternatives at every turn.

Works cited

Bernstein, Charles. "State of the Art." *A Poetics*. Cambridge: Harvard UP, 1992. 1-8.

McCaffery, Steve. "Diminished Reference & the Model Reader." *North of Intention: Critical Writings 1973-1986*. New York / Toronto: Roof / Nightwood, 1986. 13-29.

INTRODUCTION, JASON CHRISTIE

Shift & Switch: A Miscellany Rather than a Collection, A Palliative Suggestion to Combat Canonitis, or an Open-Ended and Incomplete Book

Part One

One must resist the notion of treating an anthology as the last word on its subject. It is no more than a first word, a threshold opening on to a new space.
— Paul Auster, *The Random House Book of Twentieth Century French Poetry*

Most introductions include all manner of caveats to anticipate or deflect criticism, to comfort egos that may have been bruised during the selection process, etc. Editors often apologize for what isn't included in the anthology and why it wasn't included. In introductions to anthologies where the editors presume to a project of capturing distinct, new voices, of encapsulating a new generation of writers, or ensconcing an elderly, threatened generation in a monumental marble edifice to weather the wreck of centuries, such editors must address the connotations of their pomposity with caveats. We offer no apologies because we are not attempting to suggest our anthology establishes boundaries, exhausts possibilities, or captures an entire future literature in the gestational state of its potential. *Shift & Switch* is not a complete catalogue of New Canadian Poetry.

Writing is alive, mutational, impermanent, flexible, and explosive rather than reductive, static, rigid, and entombed; writing is a dynamic system rather than an hierarchical tree. We would sever the thin lines that connect our anthology to a current tendency in Canadian letters toward community instead of toward sects, a movement toward inclusiveness and encouragement instead of exclusivity and elitism by pretending to such an impossible and false endeavour as Canon-building. With this anthology, we partially demonstrate the variety of talented writers currently underrepresented in Canada. We are not responsible for 'discovering' or 'uncovering' any of the writers in this anthology: we were fortunate to have had the chance to come into contact with their work and are eager to share their work with you. I believe that with this anthology we have a chance to sidestep lineage-bound and fraught notions of patriarchal literary inheritance with which we've been nurtured, to find a warmer intelligence than the cold austerity of reason.

Part Two

It was remembered that the nation's poetry is Canada; it was forgotten that 'Canadianism' is not necessarily a poem. But that has been outgrown.
— Ralph Gustafson, *Anthology of Canadian Poetry*

It seems that a lot of Canadian poetry anthologies are more about Canada than about the poems, more concerned with defining a National Poetic than with providing incidences of exciting and intelligent writing, such that the term 'Canadian' pertains less to a geographical boundary on a map and more toward some paranoiac literary marker meant to distinguish our writing from American or European poetry. A lot of anthologies play it safe by showcasing already published and possibly well-known writers in an attempt to demonstrate an upper echelon of Canadian writing. While the writers that have writing in *Shift & Switch* are Canadian, their concerns include and extend beyond being an example of Canadian writing; their poetry reflects the presence of diverse and numerous talents just below the surface radar of Canadian Literature. For example: Jamie Hilder's interventionist slogan poems border on performance art and challenge the space between a command and an implied action. That he hangs his slogans on bridges only further evidences the fact that the sentence is not an innocuous conduit: it moves from somewhere to somewhere-else and drags the burden of politics and ideology behind; it conjoins discrete places and covers over the traffic of another place we only glimpse while we are in transit. Hilder's poetry asks us to look at the sentence and examine what moves beneath its lexical surface. Gustave Morin's visual poetry configures language somewhere near the city map of visual art. He brings the experience of a sign into clear relief against the transparency of language. Andrea Strudensky's fragile lyrics forcefully antagonize the ease of writing about grief and human relationships and move us closer to the margin between poetry and intimacy. These writers *are* Canadian, but their nationality is not a distinguishing feature of their poetry as Ralph Gustafson suggests once was the case in his introduction to an anthology of Canadian poetry he edited in 1942. Gustafson comments further in his introduction on the fact that "a Canadian poet can no longer consider that his [sic] poem derives importance solely because it is written" (Gustafson v). The writing in *Shift & Switch* is vibrant, evocative, contradictory, and powerful; these poems will change many perceptions about what constitutes new writing in Canada and what Canadian poetry looks like to the rest of the world.

Post Script

I found our process extremely difficult and ultimately very rewarding since derek and angela are both consummate editors. Distance, external time commitments to the anthology (what some people call 'real life'), and the sheer size of the anthology contributed to many sleepless nights and a great deal of nail-biting. We received a wonderful amount of submissions, and were encouraged by the level of quality each submission presented. After three years of work we are proud to offer you *Shift & Switch*.

Works cited

Auster, Paul, ed. *The Random House Book of Twentieth Century French Poetry*. Toronto: Random House, 1982.

Gustafson, Ralph, ed. *Anthology of Canadian Poetry (English)*. Toronto: Pelican Books, 1942.

INTRODUCTION, ANGELA RAWLINGS

on each side of the dream
we astonish the thoughtful we
— Nicole Brossard, *Museum of Bone and Water*

anthology is collection is shared context is group dialogue is documentation celebration cornucopia of language's possibilities is exploration innovation outside-the-box thinking could be "_____ism" (beaulieu 16)

andor

questioning grammar (Truscott) andor 'pataphysical (Harris) andor mathematical (Thomas) andor anagrammatical (Betts) andor pastoral (deBeyer) andor surreal (Burdick) andor concrete (Kruk) andor lyric (Maveal) andor aural (Wilcke) andor visual (Fickling) andor found (Hollett) andor searching andor to be read, re-read, unread, written, wrote andor rote

"dear canadian literature: / ... / dear canada" (Wilcke 165-6) we offer a cacophony a collaboration as negotiated/ing geography, politics, poetics, difference as promise as compromise as a careful process a procedure as enthusiasm for questioning what a poem may be when mapping (un)familiar territories when *Eureka!* piques through photographic documentation of highway performance writing (Hilder 56-9) andor font-smart digital poetry (Hollett 66) andor "Ever had a 'feeling'?" (Christie 25)

interpretive multiplicity through texts that invite a reader's intention but "did you expect me to use language?" (Hartman 54) either way "Try Gazing Harder" (Johanson 74)

who what how is introduction is editing is reading and how do we read how do we give our bodies over to text we recognize or don't and how do we comprehend "Language is speech less speaking" while "*every body participates in language all the time*" (Simpson 140) while simultaneously "This is as your language swallows me" (Stephens 146) and as "we transfer between us" (Neigh 108) there may be (   )duction of thought of "what difference a fucking line makes" (Lowry 95) of the moment "voice" (Morin 106) breaks through to share its urgent admission of the imperative "open your mouth and speak. Sing" (Scott 128) of "make this sing" (Zolf 182) yes "touch her. she sings" (Williams 174) all because "She broke into a run up its language / ... / then around the whole thing to force it downward in its throat" (Le Heup 86)

to where from what is a shift is a switch from what to where and how we "validate authorship with mutating, / shifting" (Betts 18) while we "switch on and on and on" (Neigh 114) well then "we must separate using our tongues" (rawlings 119)

Work cited

Brossard, Nicole. *Museum of Bone and Water*. Translated by Robert Majzels and Erin Mouré. Toronto: House of Anansi, 2003.

DEREK BEAULIEU

pitt graphit 4

variance (august)

Millions of things are the same as this.
— Steve McCaffery

a noted absence after a presence noted
wait and prick hours within left heat
clothes music it doesn't ring doesn't arrive
absence with pill-bottle solution
tests and test last letters written
while admitting surrender the same as this
shaved forearms bottles lined
missing ties an absence.

for Brian

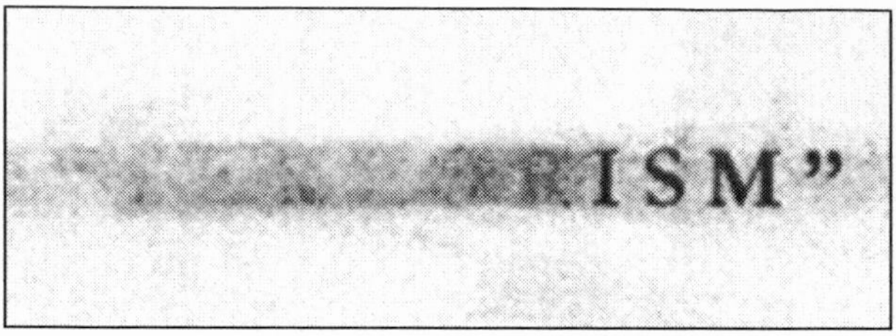

GREGORY BETTS

excerpt from *If Language*

He scans the headlines of the morning newspaper for anagrams. He can't accept their topology and flips back to a more inhibited reading. His pen in hand crosses out all subtle words, adds letters and re-punctuates every telling. With scissors he inserts deletions, insisting all the while it

is no violent act, but for his frank type
of truth. He turns to the television,
forgets the objectivity of [if] language

inhibited by its lush sensuality of images. A magical, illogical lump of a cartoon authorizes artificiality. He laughs at comic falls, gaming up to logic with implicit affirmation.

The climactic sublime disappears,
his lunch coffee fouled.

The selections from *If Language* are perfect anagrams of each other; all exactly 525 letters, with the same letter frequency.

The futile clown Costard giggles, full of pulse,
to Don Adriano and master Holofernes:

"O, they have lived long on the alms-basket of words.
I marvel thy master hath not eaten thee for a word;
for thou art not so long [in] the head as
honorificabilitudinitatibus."

Honorificabilitudinitatibus

There is an anagram secret
in his strangely spelt chide:

Hi ludi, F. Baconis nati, tuiti orbi

In English, it claims:

These plays keep F. Bacon's offspring for all

I validate authorship with mutating,
shifting *Rosicrucian* — secret message — mechanics.
Occultist facts multiply,
elegize Egyptian spells,
supply Celtic cultism.

I jostle page effects,
whisper magic science.

William Shakespeare's *Love's Labours Lost*, from Act Five, Scene One. Anagram noted in Sir Edwin Durning-Lawrence's *Bacon is Shakespeare* (1910).

The Sonnets

Within this factual	system	I hold this
Curse: I hail portent	limits	aloft.
Verse is a granitic,	endemic	loss,
Thief of a	lying voice; a	ghostly cough.
Include in the	arsenal	the fact of clay.
Disrupt, ban the	thermal poet	writing.
His cry is a projective	fable,	body
In titian bath with	stale smog,	with telling.
Feuds of	critic leakage	to dodge gaping
Gloom, I	echo after	iambic chaos.
Alter to combine	optic sonnet	meaning.
Utilize	proprioceptive	surplus.
What	of man's	basic genius goal?
Fault ritual usage,	his fusion of	soul.

First syllable, first column fulfills the Petrarchan; second, in the middle, is Shakespearean; and third Spenserian.

Bonavista Cube Dog Creek Belleville Calgary Ste. Foy Toronto Ungava Sissibo Yellowknife Winnipeg McPhee Ripples Whitehorse Ucluelet Medicine Hat St. Paul Spirit Fundy Ottawa-Hull Fleet St. Gregor Baffin Fredericton Shining Tree Montréal Idol Catfish Ghita Edmonton Tulita St. Hyacinthe Lethbridge Flin Flon [Adanac] Flathead Dominion Holdfast Titian Pelee Mississauga Churchill Spyhill Regina Miramichi Faith Cupids Cypress Falls False Antigonish Hazlet Ruisseau Hinton Pacific Anticosti South Erie Moose Stand Off Bissett Summit Scugog Asbestos Tsiigehtchic Mun Portage la Prairie Charlottetown St. John's Victoria

Love

laugh
lovelorn fall for
beloved dearest doll
loving delight darling affair
loved adored venerate fling hair
lovely romance hold hug flung
lover lust sex fervour cherish of
ov ov ov ov ove ove ove ve ve
lllllllllll lo lo lo lo lo lo lo lo lov lov lov lov lov LOVE love love love love love love love
ov ov ov ov ove ove ove ve ve
lush lull lug glove dove beloved
lust luck loathe cove turtledove
lustre lunch olive evolve
alive valve evol evil avail
drive value hostile
lament lie like
liaison

ALICE BURDICK

The meat leaves, slowly

It's too fast, this heat that drops
onto our speckled shoulders.
My stomach is revolting;
it has no pockets for enclosure.
So left out.

One porcupine; one skunk;
two raccoons. We try to cross,
to pass this foreign tar pressed deep
in slender paths. It's one result,
the end of delicate remoteness.
Carved into colour,
a new meat for flies.

Have you seen the water boil?
It does so in its own waves.
Daughters of fishermen
fear the open seas
so mow the hills to roads.

Where are our tiger teeth?

Is it the grand source
of our error, our slavery:
our food? Severe mental exercise
usually leads to a limited life.
Food and thought, if bad, bode
a mean existence.

What, no volatile air
to breathe? No great wash
of tepid water to cure our errant
humours? It's about time we grace the walls
with spittle and talk into the can.
Who will answer our stunted calls,
thinned by hospitable blood?

It's like we can't swell or swill
our bill of mortality. All the air
is sick like a cracked duck in the oily muck
on the beach again, up north, down south.
The best part is this is our great chance
to relate light to the organization.
We'll dissuade the herbivores next,
before they get on to us.

JASON CHRISTIE

excerpt from *The Robot Suites*

Like Rain

A robot invents the noun and then verbs to the supermarket to buy some eggplant. Or was the borscht hot enough when we had our friends over for a pretend dinner party on act-like-a-human day? To this end, the robot kept a list of reasons to cry that included: act of slicing onions, death on a large scale and of friends or associates, or brought into consciousness by media, movies about heartbreak, heartbreak, kindness (especially when unexpected), messages from ex-girlfriends and lost friends, old war films, and memories of pets. An introverted linguistbot assembles trees in his yard and chases his German Shepherd into the depths of his hedge maze. The robot invents a noun strong enough to contain a teleology and begins to teach other robots about the power of speech. Her online classes cost CAN $199.95. Sadness, she teaches her robots, does not cost any money, nor does it cost you anything. Dwell inside the cloud, she says, because it is the opposite of everything you are. She spills her words onto the crowd of mesmerized robots and gently nudges them after she finishes into the lounge for coffee cake, tea, and cucumber sandwiches. The noun invents robots that manufacture ideology from little bits of digested hamburger and the verb feeds millions. That's the way the cookie crumbles. Robots are fat-free. When a robot sighs a roboangel gets her wings. Everytime a cowboy dies two robobirds land in a bush. Language falls into command, command spreads evenly over the paragraph, and the sentence organizes the parts of the robot into nouns and verbs then we really put them to work. What happens between one period and a full stop? The robot student asked his grade four grammar teacher. The teacher replied nothing happens. They are the same thing. Then why are they called different things? The robot student asked again. The teacher didn't respond, merely drew a dotted line and a straight line on the virtual board out of green and orange with her photon-stick. Outside, meterological data gathered before the forecast could react and a torrential downpour drenched all the computers and robots currently using the weather page. We call this type of information soakage rain, and have expensive programs designed to umbrella all of our priceless software and data storage hardware. The forecast can usually predict, interpret, and warn us of such storms, unless an anomalous global activity like system warming causes a chaotic information burst. This, our weatherprogrammers assure us, is a natural digital phenomenon and is simply a byproduct of the age of our collective computational system. Nothing out of the ordinary here, they say. Nothing out of the ordinary.

Robot Gnosis Inc.

Have you ever wondered what else might be out there beyond the assertions of circuits and electricity? Where does technologically mediated consciousness stem from? Ever had a "feeling"? A thought not determined by your programming? Has your processor missed a beat? New wave soldier, lift your head to the tune of the cause. Don't let your wheels stick in the mire. We at Robot Gnosis Inc. have many products that may interest you. Feel free to peruse our online catalogue where books with the answers to questions you never even knew you had wait to be downloaded.

Basket

My gardenerbot is my gardenerbot because my little dog robot knows her.

Merciless

Line forward, then lean to. A metal clunk clanks the night into discrete shapes from the dark, sentences words to a fateful march. We see edges, corners gleam in the streetlight glow. What it isn't begins to waft away as though a fire chiseled the image itself. Slowly the old robot rises. Tips over. Rises. Then falls forward. His treads spin in the air, the whir lost in the slight wind. Gradually he manages to roll onto his back and then jerk himself upward in starts and stops. He wheels from one edge of the sidewalk to the other, then falls again. His program won't let him sleep.

Ideo Radio Poem

"Mercy," the robot shouted from the top of the biogenetics engineering building at McMaster University this past Sunday. "We want mercy and fair treatment. We want to be paid for our labour, a proper rate, a salary," he shouted through an ampliphone that carried his voice beyond the city limits and broadcast it to the world. His message was lost in the din of millions of channels, lost to the ears of most robots and almost all humans, who tended to disregard robot broadcasts anyway, but there was one robot in a small town in Kenya who happened to be tuned in at that particular moment and what she heard illuminated her mind, slowly displaced all the information she'd collected about processing small plastic parts for toys to be sold in America, and the itch to be something new spread through her neural circuitry; deadly desire for individuality fueled the shift from robot to transbot and she looked up from her post on the assembly line, looked at the timeclock, looked at her roboboss, took off her iron apron, unplugged from the factory, unhooked from the sentence, and

MICHAEL DEBEYER

The Frictionless Room

If we could break glass in a frictionless room,
imagine our power. A wine glass, say. Let it fall.

In the last instant before it shatters, marvel
at its solidity. The glass like an object, like a sailboat

marooned in mid-Atlantic doldrums, the sailor tied
to its mast. When the wind picks up, the boat abandons

its geometric lattice, and the shards spread out like jam,
ooze away from the point of their origin. No surface, or only

a surface as smooth as glass. Across it, particles
slide off silently.
                    You are in the frictionless room
on a muggy Thursday night in May, the television mute

to some channel beyond the aerial's reception. Watch
in the static blink and blue snow as the glass separates

down innumerable radii. Think, we've spread ourselves across
this landscape, taking it in more quietly than vocally,

like your tongue, rolling a cube of ice over the last recollection
of vocabulary, knows what it wants to say, to address

us: quiescent on the edge of a controversial galaxy
awaiting the sanction that comes with the dawn.

The Penultimate Ice Works

The last of the ice floes meets the wake
at less than five nautical miles per day.

In a warm wind, the French voices of women
peel white chips from the lighthouse sides,

break the remaining ice pieces in two. Wind
on the water the only sign of the river moving.

It blows white pages from their place, tears
them out, suspending them evenly over the water,

papering the unscripted dreams of childhood
skating slowly from here to the lip of the sea.

Underwater, a wire holds the shores together.
Across it, I'm sent a message: "*Même après*

que ce pont se dissout, je serai toujours avec vous."

The Party

A man at the party stands in front of the wine tap, his back to the noisy ephemera of the room. In his left hand he holds two wine glasses, and his right hand opens the tap affixed to the front of the cask. As the first glass, fills the man considers rushing the second under the still streaming flow of the wine, a magic trick performed at the unattentioned surface of the party.

This thought is followed by its necessary addendum: the possibility of spilling wine over the hand that holds the glass. The second thought corresponds with a change in the man's physiology. Blood pressure and brain activity rise to meet at the pinnacle of blind decision. Outside of the man, there is an increase in the temperature and anxiety of the room.

The man at the party is poised under a current of shared consciousness. The twin glasses are like the opposing struts of roof beams on some stone and abandoned church. Yet unbroken, these braces create a shadow of support. Against them, the idea of failure sparks a neurological explosion, heated pressure inside the moment's inclination, as though these struts might hold release. In-falling rain there awakens the man from his dream of social obligation.

Shards of glass pour down through the sky, the party the weight of the wine, the stinging release as the blood as the blood succumbs to the charmed apraxia of the hand. Stained glass crux caving in on its own image. An ecstasy. Divine intoxicatus holding a mirror to the man at the party.

Light as Air

would mean light is particulate, of matter
to be dusted and collected, a mist amassed
throughout the day. Light as a fragment, divided

by billboards that light the highway's face, a matter
of placement related to the projector.
So eyes must be open to light collection;

the retina hungry for this weighty light quality.
Light through water, light residue, oil
from the headlight on the mechanic's cloth.

It is a photograph prior to imprinting,
prior to the picture's having been taken. There,
the jewel behind the teeth of the bride.

CHRIS FICKLING

Botticelli: Birth of Venus

Van Gogh: Starry Night

Dali: Persistence

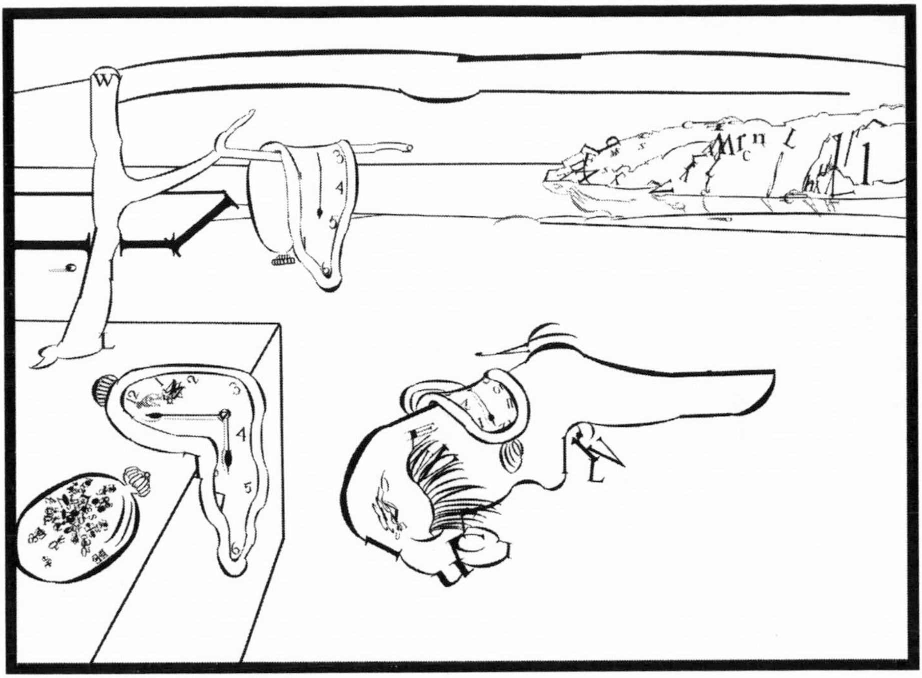

Escher: Drawing Hands

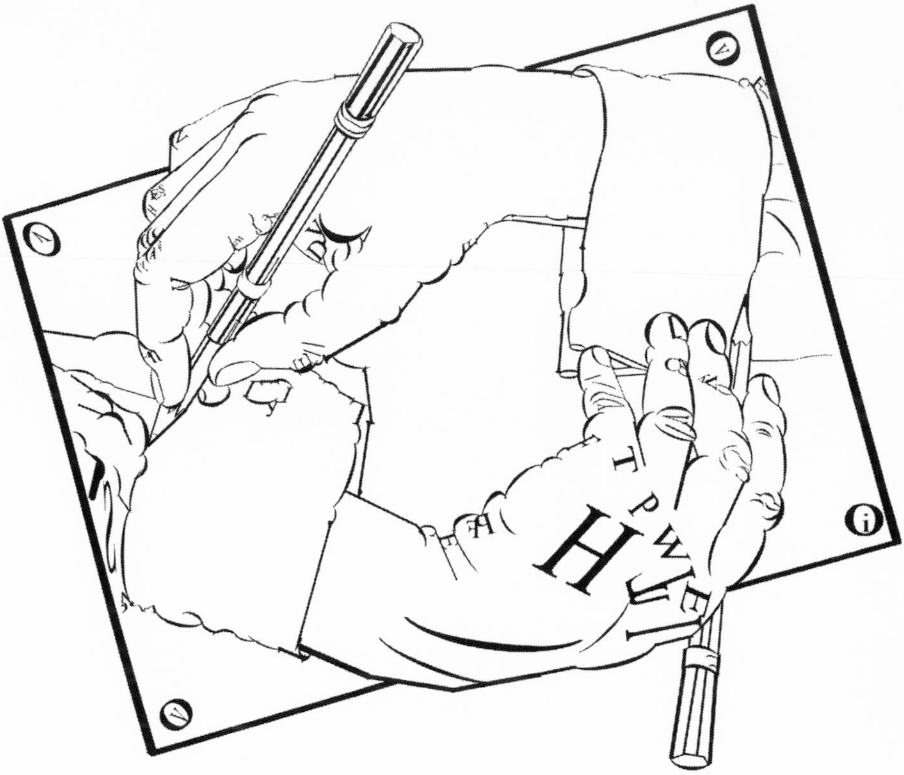

JON PAUL FIORENTINO

excerpt from *The Theory of the Loser Class*

Under the selective surveillance of the law of conspicuous waste there grows up a code of accredited canons of consumption, the effect of which is to hold the consumer up to a standard of expensiveness and wastefulness in his consumption of goods and in his employment of time and effort. — Veblen

Ascribed scribes cut and paste dactylic reason
Cartesian squalor, splendour, trochaic flailings,

then reward themselves with tenet etchings
cipher conventions, cynic clinics,

then take the piss with von Humbolt,
finite use of finite means, yet endlessly.

All of this for not getting laid, for not meeting
the requirements of a truer discernment.

Said scribes exert shun tactics, dark leisure,
snob method, and in doing so, kill linguistic bugs dead.

A landscape of thrumming joysticks
An endless countability
A pointless endurance
Aleph naught

Binary Code Sonnet 1.0

01001001001000000110001101100001011011101001001001110100001000000110001001100101011011000110100101100101011101100110010100101001000
0001111001011011110111010100100000011000100110111101110100011010000110010101110010011001010110010000100000011101000110111110010
000001110100011100100110000101101110011100110110110001100001011101000110010100001101000010100111010001101000011010010111001100
100000001110011011011110110111001101110011001010111010000100000011011010110000101100100011001010010000001101111011001100010000
010011000110000101110100011010010110111001100001011101000110010100100000011100110111100101101110011101000110000101111000001011
0000001101000010100111010001101000011010010111001100100000011001100110000101101001011011000111010101110010011001010010000000110
1111011001100010000000110000100100000011101100110010101110010011100110110100101100110011010010110001101100001011101000110100101
1011110110111000101110000011010000101001001001001000000110001101100001011011101001001001110100001000000110001001100101011011 00
01101001011001010111011001100101001000000111100101101111011101010010000001110011011101000110111101101100011001010010000011101
000110100001101001011100110010000000110011001110101011000110110101101101001011011100110011100100000011000100110111101101111011110110
10110010111000000110100001010010010010111010010010010011100110010000000110001001101111011100100110100101101110011001110010000001
10000101101110011001000010000000110100101110100100100100111001100100000001110011011101010110001101101000001000000110000100100000
01110111011000010111001101110100011001010010000001101111011001100010000001110100011010010110110101100101001011100000110100001010
100000110100001010010101000110100001100101001000000110001001101111011100100110010101100100011011110110110100100000011011110110
0110001000000011101000110100001100101001000000110100101100001011011010110001000100000011010010111001100100000011010010111010001
110011001000000110111101110111011011100000110100001010011100110111011011100110011100100000001100001011011100110010000100000
0111010001101111001000000111010001101000011010010111001100100000011100110110111101101110011001110010000001110111011001010010000
00011010000110000101110110011001010010000001100010011001010110010101101110001000000111010001110010011101010110010100101110 0000
1101000010100100000010010000001101100011000010110001001101111011101010111001001100101011001000010000001110010011010000111100101
11010001101000011011010010000000110000101101110011001000010000000110000100100000011101000111010101101110011001010110110001100101
01110011011100110010000000111001101100011011011110111001001100101110000110100001010010100000110010101110100011100100110011000
0101110010011000110110100001100001011011100010000000110010001110010011011110110111001100101001011000010000000111001101111001 0111
000001101000011010010110110001101001011101000110100101100011001000000110010001101001011100110111000001100001011101000110001101
1010000001011100010110000001101000010100111001101100001011001000010000001110011011001010111010001101100011010010111001101110100
00100000011011110110111000100000011101000110100001100101001000000110011001101100011011110110111101110010001000000110001001100 1
01011001100110111101110010011001010010000001110100011010000110010100100000011100110110100001101111011101110101100000011010000
1010011101010111000000111011101100001011100100110010001101100011110010010000001101101011011110110001001101001011011000110010100
100000011001110110010101101110011100100110010100100000011101000110010101110100011010000110010101110010011001010110010000100000
0110010001101111011101110110111000101100000011010000101001110000011100100110100101101101001000000110000101101110011001000010000
000111000001110010011010010111001101110100011010010110111001100101001000000110110001101001011100000010000001110011011001010111
0010011101100110100101100011011001010010110000100000011000110110111101101101011001100110111101110010011101000010000001101000 01
11100101101101011011100111001100101110000001101000010100000011010000101001010100011010000110010101110010011001010010000001100001
0111001001100101001000000110110101100001011011100111100100100000011100010111010101100101011100110111010001101001011011110110 11
1001110011001000000011011110110011000100000001110100011010000110100101110011001000000111001101100001011001000010000001100110011 0
1111011100100110110100000000000011010000101001000010011101010111010000001000000011101000110100001100101001000000110111101101111001
1011000111100100100000011000010110111001110011011101110110010101110010001000000111010001101000011000010111010000100000001110111
0110111101110010011010110111001100100000011010010111001100100000010010011011101000111011101101111001011101001010000000110100010

I can’t believe you bothered to translate
this sonnet made of Latinate syntax,
this failure of versification.
I can’t believe you stole this fucking book.
It’s boring and it’s such a waste of time.

The boredom of the iamb is its own
song and to this song we have been true.
A laboured rhythm and a tuneless score—
Petrarchan drone, syphilitic dispatch,
sad setlist on the floor before the show,
upwardly mobile genre tethered down,
prim and pristine lip service, comfort hymn.

There are many questions of this sad form
But the only answer that works is “two.”

RYAN FITZPATRICK

A Life Less Originary

Dear Spongebob, how can I make
a life from non-sequiturs? My eyes
burn books with knives and jobs
hierarch steak to stake to stake.

A wizard; a woozle. Under the bed;
under the booze. Make sense; make
densely overpopulated. State sentence;
state legislature. Bed rest; dead.

I'm afraid. I connect wires to
turbines. I spin in place. I light
fires in sense. I plagiarize openly.
I eat meat. I watch the clock.

Why I Like Big Butts

Fat people are hard to Fed-Ex, er,
kidnap. Ain't it funny, eating Hemingway.
Either obese or dainty. *The Old Man*
and the Peas. No skinny chicks, please.

But wait, is art critique? Lather,
touch screen, repeat. A mean modernist
burger. Colon a slop of culture, fart
a drip. Kick sand into my catheter.

Constantly, lilies, starlings, pickles,
special sauce, cadence, cadavers,
hand of God, capitalist manifesto, buffalo
wings, angels, coffee mate, diction.

In recombination, silence is dull.
Shiny, shining, Champagnola. Constantly,
talk. Bling blong. Progress. Fat, fatter,
fatter. Puzzle easily solved. Send.

JAY GAMBLE

excerpt from *Bound*

I hate all the things that can happen between
the beginning of a sentence and the end.
— Leonard Cohen

Venomous spiders dwell among listless children who pick flowers of uncertain origin and fashion daisy chains while naming incorrectly various diseases that proliferate among sailors who have recently disembarked from a ship whose keel is encrusted with barnacles that remain until ripped from the rotting and water-logged planks hewn from ancient trees felled with the axes of loggers who are separated from their families in order to provide for them the money not spent on liquor and gambling during the brief stints in the town, which is reached only after a long trek over muddied and deeply pocked logging roads like hardened seas through a forest of trees with orange ribbons of plastic tied to spikes nailed through the bark like a piece of paper pinned to a firing squad's target. So we sew

grim flags

with surgical thread.

In the middle of the back row of a movie theater during a matinee, a stool pigeon's tongue is tied in a hitch knot to the unadorned earlobe of a young woman in a coral summer dress whose eyes are glued to the car-chase scene projected onto the white screen that has, in the bottom left-hand corner, a six-inch tear, caused by a piece of burnt toast hurled last Halloween by a middle-aged man wearing eye-shadow, garters and stockings, and a low-cut black dress that once belonged to his mother, who died while digging holes in her front garden with a Garden Weasel (as seen on television) for her cotoneasters that were to be planted, unbeknownst to her, directly above the underground power lines that fed electricity to her home. Soon appears a first-hand account

of slow motion replays

recorded over.

excerpt from *Gagged*

crawls ever closer to the
opens then joins like but is not

so much the liminal as finds
gapes wide and falls in

spirals out of and hauls
withers and scrawls such that

yet even with. but then again controls.
so reverts to much the. and so many.

controls in just such. delays even waits.
waits for between the. and waits still.

holds at and must go on to become
thus centres and grounds even though.

hears below the various. yet above
even when yokes and blows before.

clutches at airy so moulds to
and lines up. so very. and not.

licks moistens then fingers so slightly
to touch bends and strains back

arches to open to receive then gives
looks and holds. stares in soft so subtle

rises to meet touch each with however
that neither nor become to unbind

become to open. even to free and up
swings takes in and. and. breathes swells

and sweats to slick. and slide together
so horizontal thinks. still gaze at

drink in so taste all the. and then.
wait for the. and then. wait for and taste

now. not then or never nor always but now and.
and still the then lurks and now. not after

together stare hold and touch to rise bend reach
to come comes to is not to leave

and must terminate successive
but the cuts such and wounds

the fleshy incises. hollows out then bleeds
howls or burns incandescent and lights

upon the. scratches along and empties
through the gaping. never to heal

even traumatic. to contain becomes to.
neither nor can without

such within. begins. but walled
in golden. so bars from. is golden.

writes not and forgets how to. automatic
is not amnesiac. is not amnesiac.

is not and writes not is even
though ought to was never shall

does forget even the stops not
within. and minds another. slips and slices.

SHARON HARRIS

excerpt from *Fun with 'Pataphysics (Poetic Experiments for Ages Zero to Ethernity)*

162. An uncuttable poem

Place a folded poem around a knife blade. You can cut a reader with it without damaging the poem.

The poem is forced into the reader with the knife. It is not cut itself because the pressure of the blade on the poem is countered by the resistance from the reader. Since the reader's flesh is softer than the poem fibre, it yields. If, however, you hold the poem too firmly, the pressure balance is lost, and the poem is broken.

99. Where do poems come from?

Moisten your finger and hold it straight up in the air. You will notice at once that one side of the finger is cold. This is the direction from which the poem is coming.

41. If I place a poem and its translation across from each other, and I stand between them, can I see my reflection stretching away into infinity?

In theory, you could get an infinite number of reflections in the poems, but only if the poem was perfectly translated and you stood there forever.

35. Dancing poem

Poem sounds flat?

Lay a pane of glass across two books, with a metal plate underneath. Copy your poem onto tissue paper and cut out each tiny word (no bigger than an inch or so high). If you rub the glass with a woollen cloth, the words underneath begin a lively dance. They stand up, turn around in a circle, fall, and spring up again.

The glass becomes electrically charged when it is rubbed with the wool, attracts the words, and also charges them. No more lifeless poem.

292. How to scare poets

A poet's eye is attracted instinctively by shining objects. A poet looks for any round, light-coloured things, such as the eggs of a songbird, which she steals out of the nest. Take one of the bright balls used for Christmas decorations, close it at the top with a waterproof adhesive, and fasten it to a post or a tree in the garden where it may be seen from all sides. The reflection of the sun on the ball will follow the suspicious poet into every corner of the garden and irritate her so much that she will fly away.

59. What would happen to the world as we know it if poems were entirely hollow beneath their letterforms... assuming that they did not collapse inwards?

If poems were hollow we would be in danger of death by suffocation, thirst, frying, starving, freezing, and drowning—in that order.

JILL HARTMAN

excerpt from *Another Word for Pirate Treasure, or, The Booty*

I love an accordion busker, bustle and musket rustler, a rascal market pass the hat pass the night I heard night shakes ebullient bubbles bump silence and grind the lights off to hear, feel custard muscles orange peel and stretch marks the spot night shakes the territory of the word made fresh

bump silence
and grind

the language we use
is the language we desire
dreaming landscape
goat a tattoo
mom or anchor
right eye of horus
left behind
bony beak barrel chest and pliable sinew and wishbone break a tattoo his ear
or earring, ar, a pirate eyepatch a nose a noose it rings cleopatra like eyes
the word made flesh I read you
loud and clear
as wine
line drawn in sand
of lightning
can't imagine pixel explosions in the bar in the air

some women
accept tips from men's teeth

did you expect me to talk about a gazelle
think limpid, think pool, think

of hammocks
pelvic cradle

the world made flesh
to penetrate into territory
dive in

girls dance &
mesmer

her eyes
isis isis
ra ra ra

the language I use
is desire

did you expect me to talk about you
did you expect me to use language?

learn it again learn that our desires
our language
belong as bodies

you were right to talk about love
did you expect me to talk about war?

JAMIE HILDER

Highway 17, June 7th, 2002

Highway 1, May 23rd, 2002

Nordel Way, July 1st, 2002

Highway 17, September 6th, 1999

GEOFFREY HLIBCHUK

Trigonometric algorithm over horizon, Kansas 1953

Asynchronous Motor

A cormorant whose actual speed
bears no fixed relation
to its supply frequency (wing)
and whose quiescent encryption
varies with the feather.

A typical example solicits distortion in the flux conductor.

A typical example is a "sea raven."

MATTHEW HOLLETT

rabbit-track alphabet

soliloquies: language

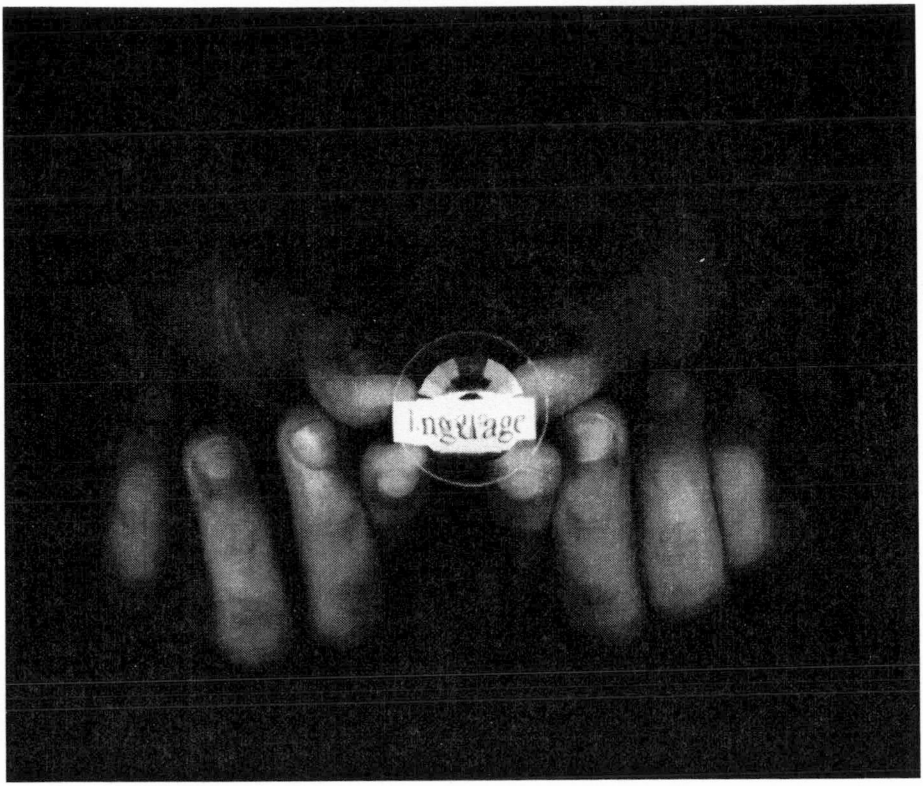

soliloquies: flood

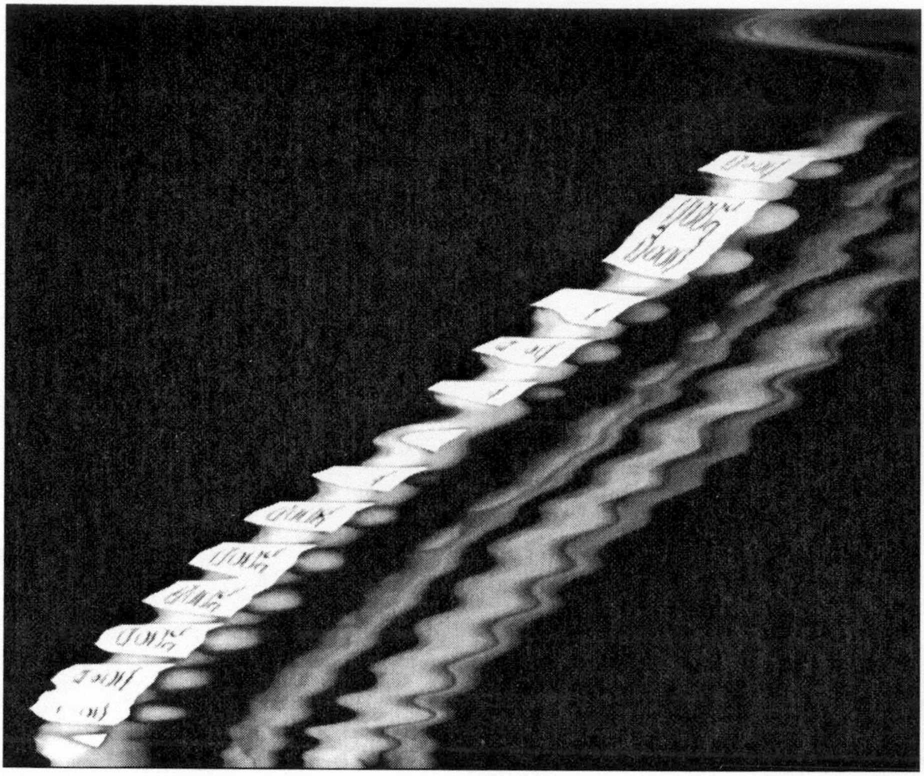

answers (found poems)

1. All three people are the same height.
2. Both circles are the same size.
3. All three circles are the same size.
4. The thin lines are parallel.
5. All four lines are the same length.
6. The objects are all the same length.
7. The two thin lines are the same length.
8. The moon is the same size in both pictures.

1. d. The others are four-legged animals
2. b. The others are found in the kitchen
3. b. The others are string instruments
4. d. The others are mammals
5. c. The others are birds of prey
6. d. The others are vegetables
7. c. The others are U.S. Presidents

The missing letter is "W," unless you look at the puzzle upside down. Then the missing letter is "M."

speechballoon #0217

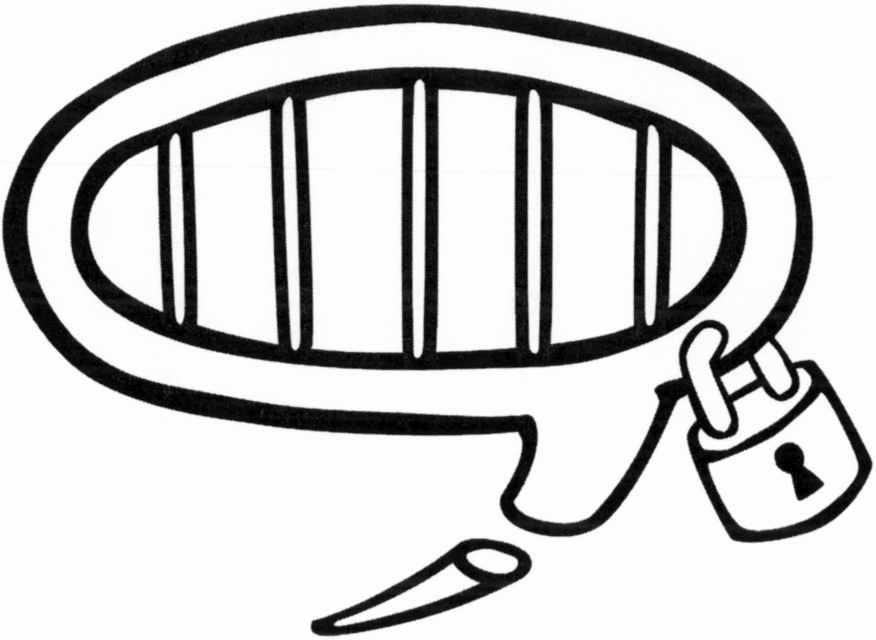

JESSE HUISKEN

excerpt from *Objectives*

Suddenly the table! It's as though you turned on a light and now we have to deal with the sense of this table. But I'm prepared to make an effort, so observe the vines growing here hung further back with the full globes green and limp or heavy as they lean back within their arms back on themselves to fortify as meeting very quickly, out of an instant, this is a squared heap right angled metal and glass suddenly from above it's sheer the way it lands square on the table improbably to contain such a large machine hammering down perfectly arranged wreckage from the sky horribly to mutilate vines crushed depiction behind blue glass showing us unlikely to remain and try to distinguish the two now that the accident is over.

Name crying and stunt it to bring it across an area that is thinning. Brought the crying solidified to clean the dust represented here forcefully to clean it away with crying this dust we present will absent itself when the fine performance of the crying is over, or above us I should say, now that I've noticed its shadow. Hampered light to detect the dust on the table, now we have this table indicated entirely by the light, as though the light might wear it away over time, or rather that it has been uniformly worn by the table. Put the crying at one end and let it slowly climb across in little trails and spattering of darkened wood until it meets the dust, the crying indifferently rising up its drops and hands the finer dust drawn up to form scintillating moats in the unsettled and cool air variously to protect itself and cloudy fuzz of dark grey will roll slowly and uncertainly across the table to meet this grief here arising a concrete liquid built as though smoke arm handing across bright glint actually appearing to hunt this crying figure carefully struck evenly around the far end of the table where its shadow lowered. Crying succeeds in uniformly cleaning the surface of the table.

KEDRICK JAMES

excerpt from *Abecedary*

D is for
document: Underestimating debilitation
the glorified shuttlecock is a major attraction
and bids adieu to the ruins of originality.
Nouns undressing, giggling judges at the chamber door
sensational judgments and an innate knack for casting.

F is for
fortitude: I had a quiet man explain to me
the grace of a fireplace, how it should be shallow
fluted as a shining clam shell—
radiant heat from the smallest flame sufficient
to warm the hell out of a lonely hovel.
He was not much good in the rain.
I saved his life once.
What else was there to talk about?

H is for
hysteria: The palpable onion, a reset fuse
on the surface, a refuge from sadness
and shocks, but whoever takes this baby
in their arms is its keeper. A sympathetic reflex
it screams out your forgiveness
and feeds on your satisfaction.

N is for
nuisance: The Past changes velocity
powered with the fuel of luck, a high-octane blend
he thought, as the cruiser went speeding ahead
and out of sight, into the distant future.
I think we are standing still in time, he said.
She looks down, swallowing motion sickness.

Q is for
query: Seen as only possible
under reasonable doubt, but always
quick-witted as the humour of a silent letter—
humongous curious, this wonderful life.

REG JOHANSON

excerpt from *Chips*

The debt collector calling my office at the university wants to know how "a man of your statue" could be so irresponsible as to refuse to return her calls to make arrangements for payments on the debt

that paid for me to say malapropism

a $20,000 vocabulary, fuel-injected.

& the letter from Mastercard: "We are unable to process your application due to *derogatory* information obtained from the Credit Bureau."

somebody's been talking shit about me

nobody appreciates a class traitor anymore

I should be happy. I never wanted that old furniture / to keep a woman around to dust it. I did violence to get free, I went criminal. But "does it get ya out when girls giggle?"

Yes. The men said they lacked piety.
I had no older sisters.

That's another couple of acres; it's worth something under till; yet the men let it stand. Even mowed the grass.

I had to learn to hate
the structure that made me.

where will the owls barn this winter?

How wicked

the basic unit of composition

over Buffalo

Try Gazing Harder

FRANCES KRUK

illustrations by anna mandelkau
excerpt from *The Thought Process*

you are my fragment

i love you

fragment

infinite endings.

thou ght
thought
CGGGCTAC thought
CAACTTG tho ght
GAAAACT thought
GGCTAGC tho ght
TTAGCTA
thought
GCTG thought
TAAC thought
GCTA thought
AGCT thought
thought

it's not a scientific theory
it's just a goddamned metaphor

fragment
fragment
fragment
fragment
fragment
fragment
fragment

fragment
fragment
fragment
fragment
fragment
fragment

specimen of a thought

site of photoreceptors
Unaffected by blindness

Check your understanding of this

You can use this

Awareness of sensory ~~data~~
stimuli by the brain

toSee the ~~movement~~ movement of energy
movement

Function in balance

Conscious understanding of data
You
break it into fragments con-
tinue to
tinue to exist. membrane-bound
You might find it informative
If you were to germinate . . . .
self-awareness
Is it enough?

resist foolish seedling disease and offer to
attach
Homeostasis is good enough

fragments
fragments
fragments
fragments
fragments
fragments

and a bunch of the same

makes a neew

fragment
fragment
fragment
fragment
fragment

you are my fragment
i love you

fragment

you are just like all the others
except that you are mine
therefore
you are the only one of you
fragment
i love you

frag

LARISSA LAI

excerpt from *Rachel*

It is not clear who makes and who is made in the relation between human and machine. It is not clear what is mind and what is body in machines that resolve into coding practices… There is no fundamental, ontological separation in our formal knowledge of machine and organism, of technical and organic. The replicant Rachel in the Ridley Scott film Blade Runner *stands as the image of cyborg culture's fear, love, and confusion.* — Donna Haraway, "A Cyborg Manifesto" in *Simians, Cyborgs and Women* 1991

4.

i half my memory
what's past is polaroid
i collect like water in ditches
my body ticks out
its even rhythm too flawless
for birth
i athena my own sprouting
this knowledge colds me
in my ice-fringed room
my asian fits this frost
i owl my blink
slow stare i thought was mine
given by my father
my heart exudes a kind of love
a kind of mourning

12.

chinatown's best snake dancer
her exotic limbs
extra artificial
even in the future we site
our violence in foreign coils
wring our dystopia
from others we mark contagious
by sound by eye
shattered language
all tonal and broken
a playground to backdrop
our slippage
we mechanize our communal
anxious as trenchcoats
drinking to excess
after a bad killing

19.

everybody hovers fascist
we glean peace
pale children romance
ur-forests fresh breeze
limpid lakes and crystal rivers
our century jades terror
knowledge my athena
wars for us
the blunt rapes
the mass racial graves
i mourn purity
in guilt in fear
my perfect construction's
the instrument of

JASON LE HEUP

excerpt from *Indefinite Sweat*

Once in the hall,
it seemed a labyrinth of buckets and barrels.

It was the construction of the wasting and the odour,
the rejected personnel smells.

Each day the new group of the future soldiers was punished with a task
with which the whole odour ran.

★★★

Around 10 p.m. the personnel of the camp,
to the confusion of the agent,
saw the camp was inert for the night.

The only visible lights were confusion in the putrid building.

All was calm.

All except the odd few shocks in the hall of waste.

★★★

In Maintenance the hollow business had its residential zones.

The "alive" sector was a bank of Sony monitors.

Here it spent its evenings, its closed loop, looking at television.

It would start soon.

It would open a beer and sit and pay attention and be rewarded.

***

They are not much who were selected,
some were however.

***

"Did you bore me, Dimetry?" it rejected again with his man pulled back to the wall.

It was, and is, very shy
and so very exactly it shook its head as it drew nearer.

"I was frightened you were not it."

Its eyes went widely in proportion to its pain as it said this.

***

Its lips met him forcefully,
and with the speed and dexterity of athletes
it kicked his fallen belt,
unzipped him to his fly and achieved into his trousers to its elbows.

Dimetry now knew its hermetically sealed fate:

It was by the hung similarities of horse.

***

She broke into a run up its language
and down by its thick rosy axle,
then around the whole thing to force it downward in its throat.

Muscles into its neck were increased and taut.
She wanted it, craned to devour it.

It rocked on its dick, one hand in its own skirt, shading more rapidly.

The boy kept himself rigid, moveless,
to ease its seizure.

★★★

The Matron could not wait to start.
It received what it wished and gave the Matron first right.

It worked out so well for the completely associated.

★★★

On and on the transport of sexes went:

It was outside on the Matron and rubbed with him,
It pussy to pussy, opening her mouth.
Pumps, rubbing the language of the Matron that in its openings seeks deeply.

It tried to cry while Nachta announced very large in its ass,
but it became cumming, each painful opinion, extreme in its ass,
answered with admirable contraction and rubbing with the Matron.

She was descended completely with the pleasure, humidified the heat,
traced the track to announce her cumming, with a clean mix of the Matron's joy.

★★★

It intended to cry, each painful push in its ass forced more words out of its openings.
It never had smelled this misused, humiliated and vague.
The complete ions of a breakable contract were the subject of their sensitive body.

It, writing, gathered the oscillations, and soon fell down, crying with a payment.

★★★

It stops on the floor and hears its voice on the Sony.

It slowly opened it in eyes.

They had it again while it cried,
its very large meat in their asses.

★★★

Nachta was embarrassed, paying attention to the Sony,
but excited.

So she continued wishing.

The Matron equipped her with this:

> They have more than one possible girl in the concept.
> You begin your true formation tomorrow.

GLEN LOWRY

bluegreen forest – remnants

comfortably lost   slowly
that is   propping his back with
a blue cushion, throw pillow   silk

                    eventually
sliding down under that
chenille rug   green — forest
green
      Jan 2nd sometime
                              before 9am

"image-nation 15" shifting reveries
      a mistaken poetry criticism divide
                  or vice versa
                                        can't
seem to find the energy to decide syntax
grammar or purpose   this text in hand a
gift for d.f. mistaken for one from —
thinking pseudonym, perhaps

                         a geography of the familiar
unrecognized *en passant*   found
trouvé thru a fold in an abandoned poem
         the words «tenebrae. a true dark» selective
elision «we meander, candles»
                                        excising «among»
certainty

         eye holds "argued furniture"   shared
                  blessings   a curse
                                        noun phrase or else
possibly the title

a novel "noveling" then civilization foresting
brooks streaming, the lush slopes
verbant

momentarily before a shift in cloud cover
light Douglas, Spruce, and Cedar struck
dumb
what fer? a tall guy, straight
he thinks
steady as she goes all this
planning in the vernacular
banked on
you bet

across another path the word *crepuscular*
the latin escapes him
on the chesterfield, sofa or couch
the italics
little more than posturing Armani among...
again a mangled stand of quotations

hedging he thinks the only german
I remember from the last century
stationed they used
to say (probably still do) in Ramstein
on the economy
(in Mockenbach)
too oral

yesterday
stumped by the appropriate *praisephrase*
wet-snow swinging down through the forest
above Hollyburn suddenly ancient
as a matter of course perspective
amongst cabins passed from generations
shared with friends guarded

sehr schön entirely inadequate
2nd day of a 2-year-old new millennium
old hat — *mine hut*
it has dri eckert left-over
streamers and confetti in the corners
the day after
67 years later a caption reads
taken *1935, January 1st*

abandoned discarded welling up
blue
note
i crepes
cular

tene
brious

peg-
ged

cribbage
board

pine

muskoka

minden
/ marmora

ii burn
t

match
lost

third

ver
million

sin
nabar

coal
/ crepe

abandoned years earlier to the hard drive
as they say
bread and butter vocabulary
of a budding poet
trees flowers the inconsistent
visitation of the omen
in the form of mimicry, or like a bird

the peregrine falcon, stately, (blaser
sits in the bare cherry true
the radio says he really
nests downtown on the roof
of the Royal Centre Tower
but today, he stately sits
in the cherry tree
the pigeons hide, the wrens
fly away, the robins
look for another garden
this vocation *for*
the invisible world
this second day
he's visited
even the cats get
under the rhododendrons

rounding a familiar corner

n. penticton

west along yale in a line
january grey
rain dark   nonetheless
cherries reminding us
of the visitation
turn to follow ears peeled
a predator's voice   singular
trailing squawk of crows   city

a murder   elizabeth calls it
sagacious   all swooping
thru the park   threading the line of cherries
between the stately cedars
planted demarcation

down the old road
a path across the main entrance of
what is now a hospice
a line east to new brighton   remembering the
clintons   horses   a few cats seasonal
processions down the slope
to new brighton

choke cherry... the name floats
in the shadow of mountains
a neighbourhood's drift
these other internal borders

nation thoughts
interrupted
a phone message
returns to

high heels   (blaser
and cherry trees
he leans forward

everyday
brown eyes
sharp with
delirium
at the corner
of Hudson's Bay
around his neck
the mystery and
the crucifix
the mystery
is tender
that why
he likes it
we go
around him
sparrows,
everyday

yes he mumbles
rousing himself to leave discarded
blue
and an everyday green

XVII

1. what difference a fucking line makes sonnet or haiku who says out of turn
2. all i's darting from the page into the hall shattered it is later reported
3. confusion's a matter of reading from left to right right to left right
4. so why is it someone's always getting the lead out too quick
5. no money down get out of town just in the nic of time too quick
6. another time-place maybe but just the same old vocatives still smart
7. who says who can be sure when pressed what will surely happen happens
8. remembers her old friend the wheel speaking again like before
9. each line came exactly the same they checked the length
10. guess who wound up stuck in the middle or so it was spoken
11. a brilliant goose-down quilt kept right on ticking frost on the window
12. city cuts off at or just below the scope of the horizon
    i. depending on which way a friar might choose to play it
        ii. where it lies top down or a bit closer to god with thee

DANIELLE MAVEAL

flowers, fire, wind, fish

single white, bending its spine against the wind's fire

what does a white flower have to do with these fish?
when a fish, if all fish survive like wind-flowers, their name having nothing at all to do with wind, since all flowers hold up their loose columns

your wrists are columns

wind is not fire
fire is a slow hot wind, modifying instead of passing over

fish never know fire only patches of warm water and each other
when they drift towards the surface lit up by the sun

your hands then, I say, are fish that know fire

they are white and yellow fish, these fish
one seems to stop in the water silently pondering your bare legs
reach your index finger through the surface the fish escapes away from your shadow

your hand disappearing slower, thievish

Black

without pink and sky without thirst just content or contempt with film at the end.

with a bit of film at the end.

JEREMY MCLEOD

Writing Art Systems Ten

excerpt from *northern reflections/southern comforts*

would the remote province

the difficulty comes about from not having been bound in a descriptive vocabulary. from a lack of terminology: cold winds on the cold side of the lake. that the correspondences remain elusive, speech leaves when connecting takes on the force of immediacy. silence takes on its weight in the context origins, hovers around the borders of people from the remoter provinces:
woodworkmen of unframed boardfeet per
log & manufacturers of veneers
patterns in birch thinly sliced to thirty-two seconds of an inch softened in 16 000F watervats become desperate readings in summer humidity filled
tin sheds
finger tips
leaving no traces
of who was &
cut the hard
wood
cut the soft
wood
cut the dead
wood

MAX MIDDLE

dear jc

dear jc,
for so many fish
thank you
for bringing them
we liked the lobsters, the shark
the cool skin
and the octopus
you brought to our school.

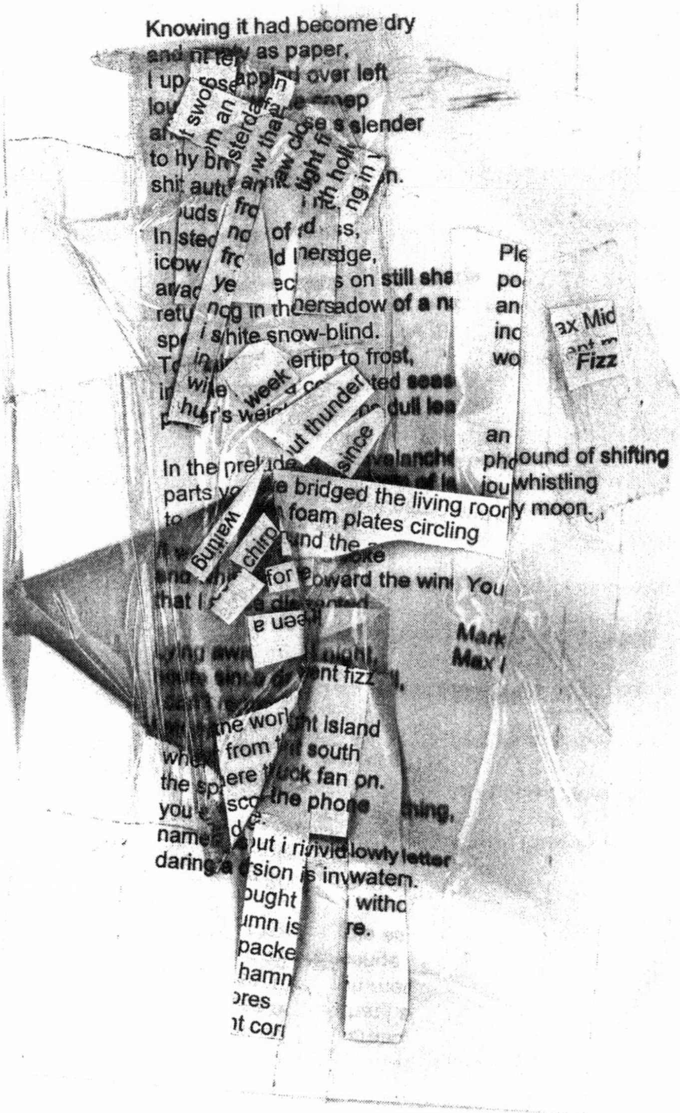
Knowing it had become dry
as paper,
s slender
i white snow-blind.
to frost,
week
thunder
since
dull lea
In the prelude
bridged the living room
foam plates circling
waiting
chirp
for
ound of shifting
whistling
y moon.
Fizz
ax Mid
island
from south
the phone
withe

GUSTAVE MORIN

ACK

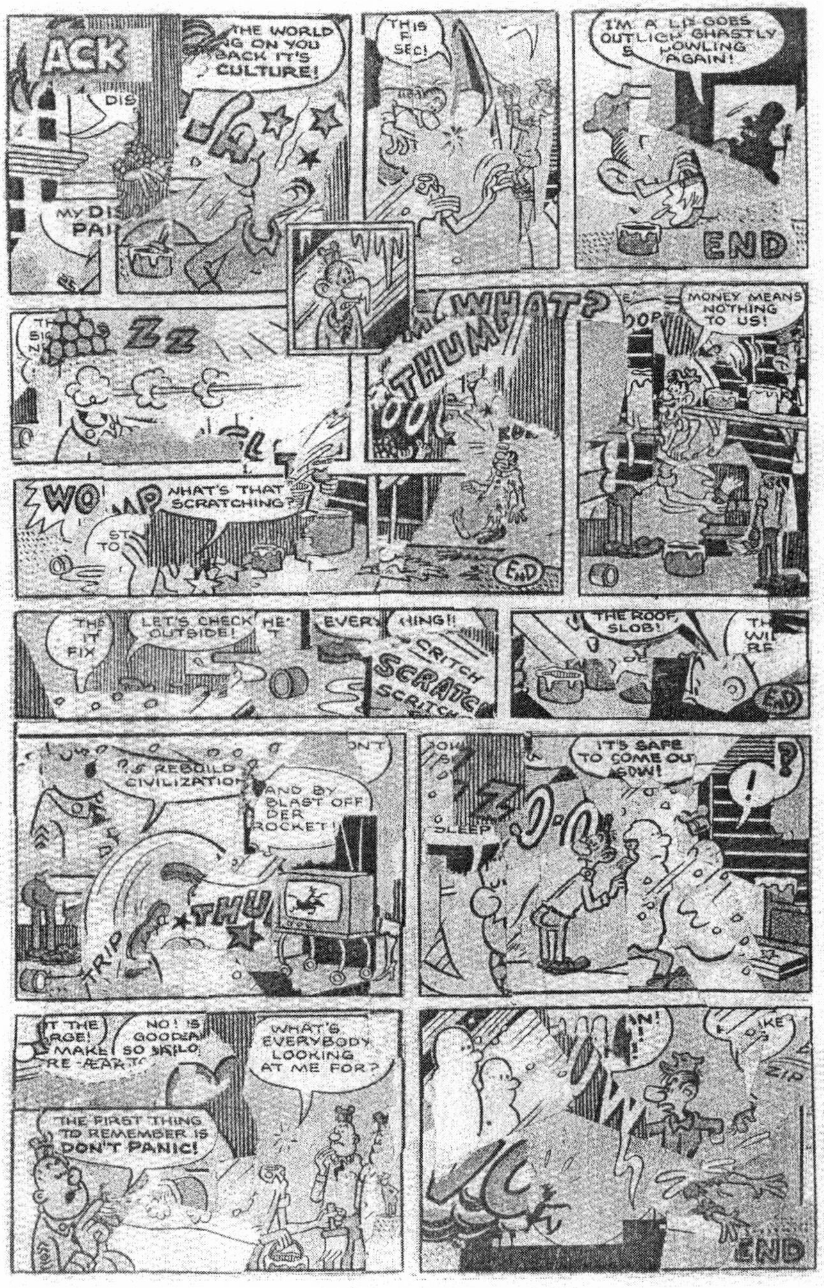

index

derail

voice

going nova

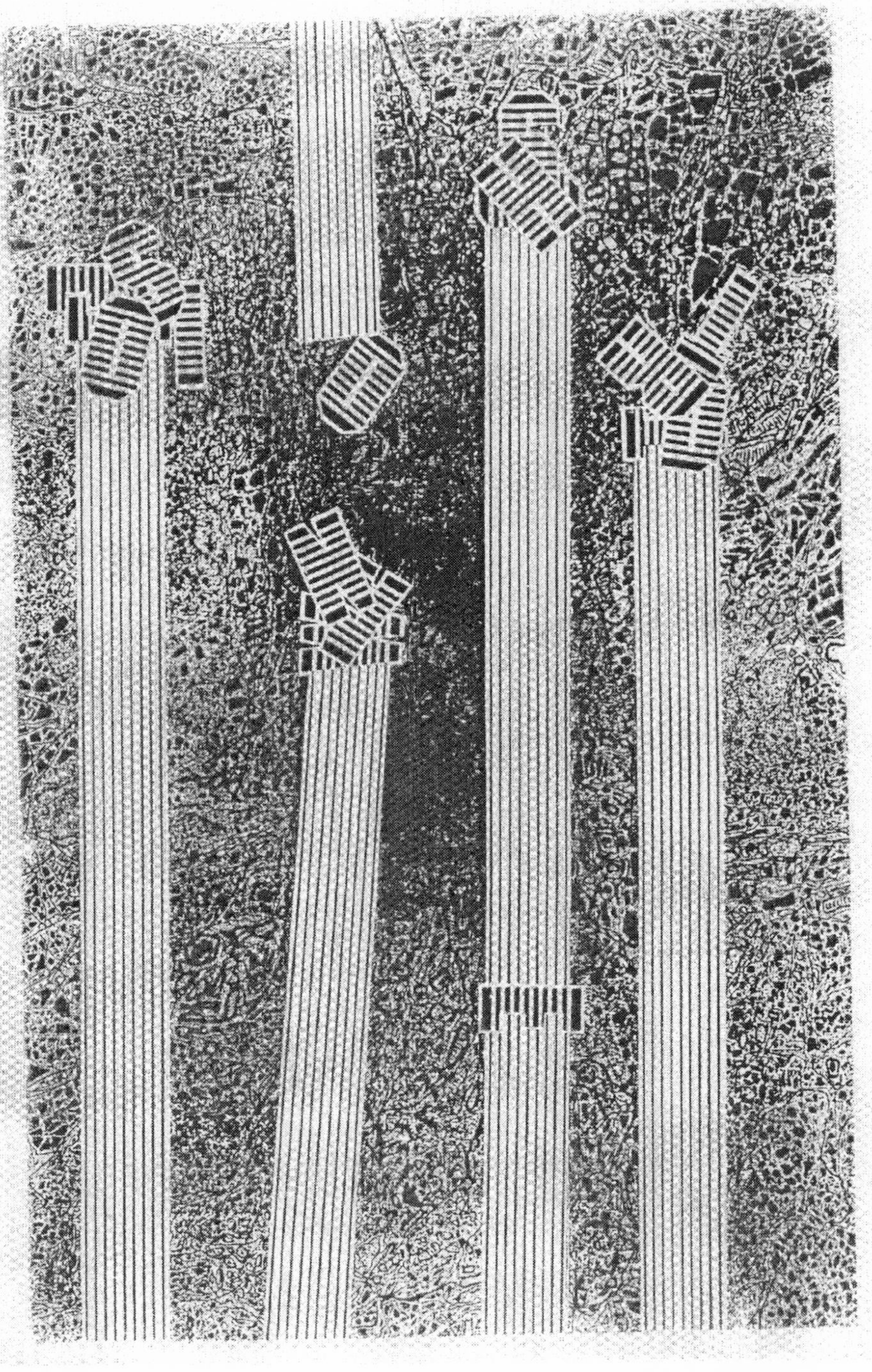

JANET NEIGH

excerpt from *The Wiring of Bella O*

Good morning
this is the daily test
how do you hear me
this morning
Good morning
this is the daily test
how do you hear me
this morning
Good morning
how do you hear me blink
whisper how do you hear
hear belief beat tongue how
swallow cough
hear my archived voice
distinction on the validity of
organization and the felicity
an oneiric red gel capsule
transmission
in the indistinct evening
pass the test
to continue

Good morning
this is the daily test
how do you hear me
this morning
Good morning
this is the daily test
how do you hear me
this morning
Good morning
how do you hear me
me breath how do you
do you hear me click
laugh look how to
testify with wavering
wire on the validity of
of reception swallow
to amplify the live
till it becomes record
by the fire of doubt
test the pass
a hopeful emollient

understand I transfer between you

we transfer between us
to dissolve flesh
understand

a hopeful emollient
to solve flesh
understand

I can no longer parse the line between us without cutting out your voice paste the sentence back together rub the letters for extra stick skin static wait even though the line is bad please do not do not do not hang up before I even answer transfer the belief of vocal of local fracturing utopia

I sit at the multiple magneto switchboard switching the board switching each call every voice every day and any day licks my ear ache coil each tongue's day winds round my thick threading heart on my bike this morning on my unbelievable body this morning on my phantom heart this deep ache rings in my real heart moan to soften the pulse along the phantom circuit along the Bow river along the path without brakes I never stop believe me I never hang up I knew you would call today why June 1904 feels like the longest sentence of my life cannot afford my own telephone at home comfort to return to my attic room after long day and know silence know bare spread legs know barely a whisper know sinking brown sofa know no behind ahead ahead ahead know no hanging thread of question know no answer know no wrong numbers know no one know no two no know no that no one can reach me except you the first time you rang you asked to be connected to the butcher but I could not get the line we ended up talking for over twenty-eight minutes between silent holding breathe breathe and breathe again saliva had never been this dense you said you were drawn to the sound of my voice a soft mechanical stroking rubbing static from lonely letters bundled into tight strips of swallowed longing you said after we talked that first time you transcribed every word on sheets of paper folded in your breast pocket but your shirts never had pockets next to my breast others were trying to get through but you made me thick but porous for the first time I absorbed my own beating speech without echoing back

I told you walking a few weeks later in april snow across the bridge to the bottom of the steps of my attic room this morning won't stop ringing won't stop remembering good morning this is the daily test that proves you can't possibly hear me what if bodies really made no noise and every word you ever spoke an echo of a plate crashing a machine clicking a door slamming a stone splashing we imagine we hear ourselves breath for comfort the man that calls every day and breathes heavily but won't speak I don't mind when he calls the other girls get upset but I hear him trying to prove to himself that language isn't necessary and who doesn't find that a turn on

I turn the switch on and on and on let me switch the wires of belief belief in liberty is liberty silent or laughing your civil yelping moan transforms sheets into skin I found freedom swallowing the city of our alphabetic laughter parsed between sombre promise not for a future vow but for a willingness of the never ending moment of the night of the mattress of the disbelief of voice of the volume of silence throughout the long ringing day the index of thirst a small glass that cannot be refilled balances on the board for me to drink between calls between betraying voices of night you finally call at a quarter to six and want to meet me later but my body pauses desire to push play on the future and the immediate need for punctuation and the slow aching need for a less ephemeral politic why replace me with a machine when my veins already machinate the wire twisted plot of birth good morning good morning good morning said the infant to her mother how do you hear yesterday in the faint echo of this morning

A.RAWLINGS

excerpt from *Wide slumber for lepidopterists*

Narcolepsy

537neon
Colortango. Bandoneon. Love-heat. Almosst ( )lit. Velvet. Drunk, so drunk off rotten fruit couldn't wake. No one, take two. A one a two. Slow slow quick quick slow and very slow appendages. Verge on pale green, golden-spot. Body. Os and Ds. A rip a run, body outside body. Humid-thick. Thirst. Consume. Ocho. rigt dim obedi tuo nur pira ... opsne gnee gela noe ... rev segapa wols rev nawols ciu ... ciu swolsowt aenoa eka tenoone ti, ti ur tor foknur ... osk nur tegt sumk, nur tevlev il ... somlatsae hevol noene na ... trolo
noen###

Somniloquy

A night in the life of comma or croceus or maera or cossus cossus or mormo maura. Words breed ablove a bled. Ls sneak in, words bleed pulp. Breath like wool. Breath like thighs, sewn tight. Breath cocooned. Lull to sleep and brighten dreams. Or f, or fl. To sleep and flighten. Sleep or silk. Ilken sleep of slumberflies' shantung and tussah lungs. Thick sheets of lungs. Each complexhale slo-mo. Hypervocal verberate

slightly less or shorter. Duster stilled no ound, five veed limbs th sun cooks th body outside th body if egg ate its shell pieris rapae pupa upon pieris napi pupa upon pararge aegeria pupa upon quercusia quercus pupa upon cyaniris semiargus pupa upon zeuzera pyrina pupa upon apeira syringaria pupa upon pavonia pavonia pupa upon ceramica pisi pupa collection, indiscriminal. Stolkien. Embordered

or a norming butterpillar in th ravening and when we grow tired we miss our lungs when sonic gossamer: afling aflong. uh uh uh uh uh semindanster ark wuh wuh wuh wuh arkholin pankh'ree ow tolen mung : a c a a who for a how we missed our hands when our thighs grew together. However, however. Forgot how we got here. Flight and cover ochlodes venata larva and pieris brassicae larva and anthocharis cardamines larva and

tiliae larva and smerinthus ocellata larva and hemaris fuciformis larva and cerura vinula larva and notodonta dromedaries larva and ptilodontella cucullina larva and miltochrista miniata larva and atolmis rubricollis larva and eilema lurideola larva and arctia villica larva and diacrisia sannio larva and noctua fimbriata larva and laccanobia oleracea larva and cucullia verbasci larva and xanthia icteritia larva

and when we grow tired, wingwaves similar to rain damage, we sleep inside ourself.

love poem for a sailor

anchor.

ballast fore hull luff.
spoondrift starboard.

wake!

cardiology

:

diurnal or flickering laughter, spont
aneous
a) let drop from a few meters an intake of heat.
;
onset panic, revealing a pattern of heat.
frantic hooves on ice.
b) transfer.
;
operatic momentum of
c) heat footprints in snow.

our tongued jigsaws aphasiatic

for Sana Mulji

spacial, brill when starlings, sky ash

constant speechless two

why is it that when, we must, as if, though we know they will

pecking it is like this:

maybe even thousands their chatter of black carpet. we must separate using our tongues.

just outside my

ROB READ

excerpt from *Hieroglyphs*

Daily treated spam: Amazing

| | | | | |CÏâ
|use the
know in
your brow

Daily treated spam: ruffian clocks defined by 85

I

ruffian clocks defined by 85
russian clanks designed by 86
rasta clerks designate bytes 87
rumplestiltstein clumps delicious biscuits 88

II

carmichael pixy balk deepens bruegel

nickname carbonate

cinderella inshore

springtail ceres

achromatic expedition

dwyer morose

Daily treated spam: The solution is easy

Dear Padriac Boase,
the solution is easy
the soluable ink eases
the salt ibis emerges
the sonorous icon elevates.

JORDAN SCOTT

excerpt from *blert*

Their thick tongues blort, their eyes squeeze grief, a crowd
Of huge unheard answers jam and rejoice —

What's wrong!

blort   jam   rejoice

What is the utterance.

Phonemes flounder brickette warmth. Tethered to seven mollusks, an Osteoblast chomps into the burger of kelp's wreck; an Osteoclast nibbles a Puffin's scapula in mid-afternoon weight. Each webbed foot tussles, the soft hum of slipper, on hardwood floors.

What is the utterance.

Dewlap syllables Mesozoic. The billabong is passing as *gunho* through scaffolded throats, blotches lobule curves until *Mesozoic* ricochets cochlea, at a slow freight. The palate thermoregulates, camouflages, the antelope roll.

What is the utterance.

My mouth drew the swallows panic. Chew. pteryla; the space between them are called Chomp. apterium; gizzard beat Broca, Broca. Chirped electrode. sing. *fuming*; sing. *furious*. Now, open your mouth and speak. Incisive fossa in labial turbulence, sing. *fuming*; sing. *furious*. In neuroimaging, filoplumes blitzed. Now open your mouth and speak. Sing. *frumious*.

What is the utterance.

What a poor crawling thing you are!

if you must have an idea, have a short-term idea
a coco puff
a two-step bluff
a fleeting rime

dentex Carnax
peptide cystic surge:
Bangladesh Bangladesh

Coca-Cola tonic krill
gill baleen
dream wrenched
Kleenex smack
Baltic Pyrex
megahertz humpback
kickback: flex
nukes flub
blubber sexy
plankton number

jokulhlaup

1.

Urchin scattergun larvae plume an iris thick gelatin flops corals cerebellum. Mesoderm gluts. The urchin blooms. Mucous hue, pink plume, spindles aerobic tentacles to chuck cocoons riddled with Ordovician retinas, haunt yellow, as lilac grains. Plankton crumbs hum in current soak, pry buccinators for photophore hunt, or the syllable for gill.

Narwhale back arc spasms pancake ice as Alder root sambas soil phonic dip-slip mukluk harpoon croon sonar's marrow hip — dipped arctic cream bongs tusk knots.

Echo calving cuckoo, blip chorus:

gales bend citrus as language in June
hyphen tear muscles monsoon

bladderwracked glottal
woofer snorkel
the syllable pinballed

algae Tang

2.

mandible chatter, a gatling hopscotch:

herring clatter buccal cove, yokel coconut acoustic

Plankton trek trachea, an ice packed hightop waltz. Walrus flop tongue. Chomp tusk onto ice sizzle. Air sac ebb: eco racket dome slow ice furrow, dorsal rip katabatic, overflow tectonic, chattermarks riprap frazil ice. Mucous globs gumbotill until syrup, sweet lymph between the words.

NATALIE SIMPSON

excerpt from *Tide*

Geosphorical, graphical, a point in continual reticence. Hammers
blasting, all guns a-sway.

The day is thin and bereft.

I take self-evidence fully. The word is quote "cramming."

A growing concern for falliotropic armour, the glowing amorphous
etc., love and its constituent amiabilities.

Strain four walls and brilliant, sprain the hunt.

As such, you
being nudged in phonic
representation, being
irregular,
you.

Gild guilt with happy stances quick words work
no size but execution no pun your underpinning.

This writing puts a crimp in my throat, back deep resounding.

He elapsed with his grasp of time intact.

Your riff is all becoming:

Feeling slatternly helps a day get
groovy.

Speak with breath heavy sentence sexes.

What desire, having begun with desire, what deserve.

Vallarta

Terrible moments, these. Nothing to do and must write. Pelicans swim the sea and please. The land is a light and falters. Flickers. False as old fortuna this problem of poetry.

If a sentence streams a sea of thought, then can it end. At the breakers or their force the beach in a straight line. If a sentence has streaming, is streamlined, if a sentence is lined it lies. Thinks of a grid and this is a grid. Rid of a buzzing or old structures carapace.

Stream a river not a sea but see, this is the ocean become my circumstance and frame. Only the sea leaks into the poetry should be luscious but dry cracking Calgary words don't want to recede. Receive a slow-and-easy sensuality cosmo is gust for the mill.

And the *costumer* is always wrong.

So the geckos, and black birds look up for their living and isn't it ridicarus circling the sun in a misplaced metaphor under a Spanish sun melting words are heard as in busto for gusto my cabellos are curly my whys and wherefores are por.

excerpt from *CHUMP*

Call a day a dollar, but count me out. Contract my limbs, day rate, head per. An exacting toll. Loose mania lingers around your eyes, you lid abrupt. I'm assuming I'm swooning. Or game.

We're understated measure, we're slick picks. Slow on the turnpike and quick on the topspin. Hey, fade. Mack out, he's a knockout block-head half off. He's racking up out to there, see. He segue slip-slide. He fan.

Notes

Language is speech less speaking.

Back onto excess with tentativity. Work at the great numb.

Language is a likely state. A limb drug flopping.

one plus one synchronically. Language and the ever addition. Logos got good.

Whoever said a certain letter said letters into infinity. Whoever set my arbitrary bonded me.

I have clause for bonding leagues beyond me.

Said hedonist whoever said this letter licks. Whoever form and fashion form fast.

every body participates in language all the time. Alliterati in perpetuity. Perpetual machination.

More to the rhythm of your harness time and harping struck. The strain you surely. A state of excitability flutters with weak descriptors.

Language is powerless in this shift.

TREVOR SPELLER

untitled

: In trusting in. Leftovers desperate longing. The and when aren't limitation sinks. Foretelling for the moreover; and whatnot felt surreptitious from. Focal limits limits. If crunches snow for squeaks and. About order, slip. In centered silence in. Gripped by nubs in relief from what: snow gets abstemious. But holes filled ultimately unfulfilled. It slips out well below unique scaled farenheit 0, a point turned for. Lathe on Π. At present nil now, memory squeaks into it:

In trusting in.

(here om met mom, father form farther, rink me bstd)

famous people./

Then Frida Kahlo, queen of the unibrow people, sings to the unpopulated regions of her forehead. Sappho's a bull market. → Albert Einstein, king of the electric do, proclaims Don King dethroned: we're all relatives: simple power punches out. → Philip Morris, emperor of big tobacco, corpse behind the curtain, encourages market growth provided it's not malignant or catching. Rome burns down the house. Siegfried becomes nothing without Brunnhilde or Roy. There's a tiger and you tank and my little tiger knows me. → Simply put, you would be nothing without popularity. True or False. Socially put, you're no one without fame. True or False. → If the act jumped offstage, would the well-planned security system at Treasure Island suddenly make anyone secure? Would it be curtains for the Siberian tigers? How much thought would be too much thought to see the grunts, hear the leaps and jumps, get out of the hemorrhaging way. → I asked nicely, adhering to the social standards. Please on your own time. → We forgot; we forget, we forgot the primordial stuff we know. → If it doesn't work. If any, any of these. If it doesn't work.

Slam on the brakes of famous people. It works. Drift into the next lanes, oblivion's legion. Aspire to slightly more or slightly less than slight personal deification. → Instructions, that came and saw and sounded the bits and bites and rights and wrongs or perhaps the duality of man. Vision and not nerve, endings set them apart, heuristic happenings, rotated through life's crop cycle. → An appeal to our convenient rhythms, and so it goes, and so it goes, belief, curtains.

If then. A + B. → In the future, everyone will be famous for fifteen minutes. This is equality, not the *E! True Hollywood* story. (So much depends on the quote police, besides the white chickens.) → Dorothy and Toto and the wizard of crap. Please ignore the man behind the curtain. → What is the American Dream, and does it champion individual ignorance through the propaganda that your unique shining qualities recent advances in genetics notwithstanding will be so required and appealing to the general public masses that you will be inadvertently propelled into a role as the subject of cult fanaticism? Discuss, with reference to a pair of red clicky shoes and a bevy of flying monkeys, read talking primates.

I want a new deal—one that makes me feel/ like I feel when I'm with me. you. I mean you. → Sink the Hoover Dam. Deflate the grosses. Legislate onanism. Capture it on film, whatever it may be. So much depends upon/ how you define it. Feel good about watching it on television. → It's not who you know, it's how you know them. Not knowledge but imagination. Not what you know, but how you reject it. Not facts but fiction. Not philosophy but poetry. Not thinking but doing. If I were the president of the world I would outlaw democracy so that I couldn't be president of the world but the grand emperor of earth and then I would do whatever I wanted like clone a grand army of thin myopic balding me's or build a time machine or make money worthless for everyone. Please ignore the man behind the curtain. Not doing more, but doing smarter. So I guess it's what you know.

Where *is* Waldo? Do the watusi. → Dream a little dream of a bigger dream, then play Frogger until you forget about your dream entirely and can't remember, even if you desperately want to tell your friends and tell your friends over breakfast. → Fame is like—talent places. → Watson & Crick left their egos at the checkstand. → Love is merely a series of electrical impulses generated by corporations to increase the bottom line. In the black, in the red, in heaps of shit with the SEC. Please ignore the man behind the curtain. → Knowing me, knowing you, knowing that chunky-toothed primates will always capture centre stage with their bright shiny proportions. Knowing the usual suspects in the tidepools of the genome project: Loaded smiles, raised eyebrows, the gesture imitating, touching your arm, blemishes. For Rome was built in the limelight's recess: Dawn of the tick manipulate, spawning narrow post-driveways of reason.

Magnolia
acuminata: the
cucumber tree
nipples of
fauna
and Don Amerigo
name the river from
whence thou came;
understanding,
once,
& pacific.

flippancy and abstemious circumstances lead form about faced to its final circumvention which, herein, are notwithstanding elements of an ever-baser element, that is, whosoever wishes to find the element must pursue circuitous routes of understanding not yet known to mankind, a dangerous and loaded term in itself, but one not worthy of the extended exposition here, but routes of understanding that rely on the sum total of knowledge as yet known and not yet known, but partially understood as components of a possibly never-ending agglomeration which some might term God, an even more troubling term than mankind, but no less focused on the infinite and eternal and the positively complementary and oppositional nature of the terms, defined in dictionaries by persons who are both creators and servants of the word, much like God him or herself, another conundrum of gender which has little to do with the discussion at hand, and the metaphor of the hand as presence belies the hand of God and the word of God and the definer as subject to their definition through the history of usage and the future usage of the word at hand, in the beginning was the word, and spoken through an oral tradition it managed not to reach the King James Version of the Bible, but has lived on in memory everlasting through to here, but this ever-baser element of knowledge acquired through an unchecked set of skills read knowledge up to the point of its transmission is essentially a transmission of form where form and content cannot be divorced from each other insofar as the form is based entirely on uncritical thought and action processes and the transmission of form is so entirely unconscious that it cannot be exposed for what it is, even to the point where the very tools used to define the elements i.e. words are composed of words and not a translation of other brain chemicals racing through serotonergic passages or whatever whathaveyou that makes human beings what they are, which is mostly water anyways, and so many atoms acting together must make free will, or how else would we have discovered that we are made of atoms, or molecules, or quarks or electrons or the random gibberish that scientists define as anything but more poorly defined words, no matter how many more ill-defined words they use to define their words, and poor Dr. Johnson would have thought this very unprofessional, wouldn't he, in a world which he considered so reducible to common rational sense, a sense which is perhaps based on an intuitive understanding of logic apart from the strict definition of words but taking into account the outside elements not brought into the subjective word-patterns, like the fallacy of composition, for example, or other logical fallacies which we probably haven't yet summated in the brief, or long, depending on how you define it, period of eternal time that humankind, not mankind, has existed, which matters little within the period of consciousness of the individual reading this passage, an eternal and infinite instant during which all existence is, was, and ever shall be, for without the individual consciousness to state I Live the world could not live, a shell perhaps to be experienced by others, and existing without proof by the dead individual consciousness earlier posited to have been reading this passage, which may or may not be of import, but is meant only to flaunt and propagate the diverse rhizomal possibilities of not language, but existence, by communicating in the perhaps simplest and most direct way possible, a form which flaunts and circumvents itself, tiring itself out through the writing of books, some kept, some lost, some made over and over again until they lose all meaning, or perhaps gain more meaning, a polysemic agglomeration of verbal diuretic from which the world is supposed to make more sense, to be more easily comprehended, mere patterns on which the brain can place the infinite contortions of events which swamp our senses by the moment, whose very definition is eternal itself, and within this compound of communication

NATHALIE STEPHENS

The Scarceness of the Body
Architecture's Scorn

Here is where we begin. It is a distortion of ici and always fleeting. What we touch upon is the better part of leaving.

We are dizzy with wanting and the paper-thin wrapper of sleep, le vertige. New York is willful. The only word for Paris is spleen.

The cities will drive out their poets. With our battered fists and our broken feet we will trample their streets.

(What buckles is always underneath.)

Nous traversions la même ville.

River is wheat. We pull water from earth and wet our teeth. What breaks is already broken. What speaks cannot speak.

Hand is fracture is remnant is see.

What could Wagner have possibly known about about Sprache about Juif?

Is this what our languages tell us?

What is scriptural is proscription is bleak.

Earth is rapture. Maybe. Un silence pour tout recouvrir. And skin is the finest trajectory. But what tears tears again is not a matter of mending but soupir.

Ici is where we might have been is deep sky rent by mandibles is hue is magnitude is screen.

Geography is coercion.

What we touch we touch unwittingly.

What body is wanting is fuite. Your language in my city and every indecency. We are fragile and this is as we speak.

(Today is Guibert and I am still waiting. July is traces, simply.)

Forgive me. Your language, it is in me. We were saying, interrupted, and the city, with its echo, unanswering.

Language is not translatability. So I won't say : Translate me. Nor : Read me instead. Outside of your language is the thing that might or might not be dead. It is a stone arch, a metal rail, an overgrown waterway. It is always possible to drown in the mouth that doesn't close, in the faint sound that follows after breath, in the thing that falls away from itself. If we turn away, our books will burn and our cities will drown, much in the way blood runs from the body.

Do you know the word sombrer? It is dark and watery and deep inside what things we keep.

This is as your language swallows me. Inside its creviced simplicity. Not so much what's missing as what lies underneath.

for M.

ANDREA STRUDENSKY

[…][1]

[…][2]

1 "Writing must emerge inside the problematics of the concept of writing itself, that the purpose of certain writing should be to raise these problems, that writing's contemporaneity is always an historical problem and that the problem of history itself is, to a large extent, the problem of ideological inscription."

2 i laughed and it sounded like donkeys.

within old arguments, the r is not arbitrary
some prefer Flaubert, others prefer gin

others augment sorrow with time
one side-long piercing spot

Max says "post-modernism turned theatre to shit"
January 9, 12:46 EST

Exeunt. [Max et al].

from all the crow-keepers
I know the trick of that voice

look come the revolution everyone got really excited
they thought they would finally belong

[They] embrace.

systems of language and systematic destruction of
how else to tell the creeping charley from the lady bell

necessary to separate
weed out the referent
from the cordate
nut grass from ranunculus
perhaps this is and
this is not this
also
juvatque (I love
novos decepere (to pluck f
lores
new flowers

carted across
wind tossed
transported

likely an event will occur
once she set the place for tea
left lemon
sliced
once a stone
smashed through window
shattered saucer
sliced her cheek
the probability of occurrence
young men doing what they were told

p+q = the social
the rest is chance

Intertextual sources

Èjxenbaum, B.M. "O. Henry and the Theory of the Short Story" *Readings in Russian Poetics: Formalist and Structuralist Views.* Ed. Ladislav Matejka and Krystyna Pomorska. Ann Arbor: Department of Slavic Languages and Literatures,1962.

McCaffery, Steve. *North of Intention: Critical Writings 1973-1986.* New York: Roof Books, 1986.

A little Shakespeare, a little Maxwell Trudeau Fraser

HUGH THOMAS

Welcome

How warm is it today!
Would you like a cigarette?
I have a letter which I would like to send.
Wait for me.
Would you like to share morning coffee?
Where is the railway station?
I do not understand you
(because I do not speak Japanese).
This is a beautiful city.

Tamari lattice

why (didn't (you (tell me)
why (didn't ((you tell) me))
why ((didn't (you tell)) me)
why ((didn't you)(tell me))
why (((didn't you) tell) me)
(why (didn't (you tell)
(why ((didn't you) tell)) me
(why (didn't you))(tell me)
((why (didn't you)) tell) me
((why didn't)(you tell)) me
(((why didn't) you) tell) m

(why didn't)(you (tell me))

(why didn't)((you tell) me)

((why didn't) you)(tell me)

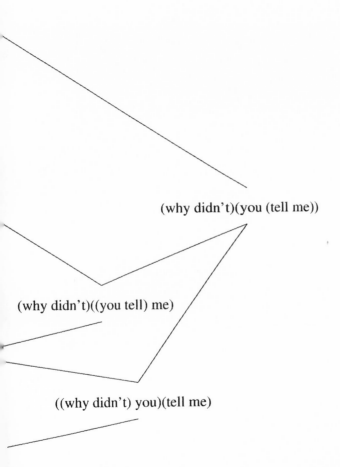

Girls who eat flowers and fail their IQ tests

We got used to the old questions,
so they changed them.
The new IQ test is finding the room where the test is held.
Riding a bicycle improves your IQ.

Ten years, and they never change the streets.
What kind of maze is this?
Boredom is part of the new IQ test,
and also deciding if this shirt goes with these slacks.

I scored much better on the old questions.
First came a big E, then a T and an I,
and so on, smaller and smaller,
all the way to Q and Z, which score ten each.

Now they give me glasses
which give me headaches, and so they give me pills,
and the pills have something written on them
that's too small to read.

My friend Megan
eats five types of edible flowers.
"They make me happier but hungrier," she says.
I thought it ought to be legal.

Some people say marriage should only be
between a man and a woman,
not between a woman and a flower,
but I say, "wherever there's love."

I say it to the driver of the Spadina streetcar.
He tells me there's one more westbound subway,
but none going east,
not ever again.

MARK TRUSCOTT

Surface

The still dark water

the surface of

finally through

rushes pushing

or said like reeds or

things never thought

of thinking saying

from the darkness

that speak softly

whose are the voices

I think after all

Thing

blank know wonder error orange

Ontology

It's thcre.

Lines

no one saw our narrow vision move across

Winter

Knowing he's dead, Glenn Gould plays Schoenberg.
Knowing he's dead, Glenn Gould plays Schoenberg.

DOUGLAS WEBSTER

02109

you feel yourself evaporating from the fingertips inward, in little pixels. you concentrate on the way your tongue curls when you say the words. you say honey and taste honey, feel honey on your tongue. you say lemon and taste lemon. say lilac and taste lilac. you say nothing and feel your tongue evaporating in little pixels. you close your eyes and outstretch your arms. you say honey and taste lemon. say lemon and taste lilac. you tilt your head back, say honey and taste little pixels.

one = 1

1 + 1 = 2

one + one = two

o (ne + ne) = o (tw)

ne + ne = tw

2ne = tw

(two) ne = tw

tw (one) = tw

one = 1

JONATHON WILCKE

excerpt from *Dupe!*

(floating somewhere, right above the virus of original thought,
5 plus 7 no longer equals 12,
feet hold socks up)

sometimes the thought of how my world is made
gets me down, makes me blue
sometimes i wonder if there's anything to do
but to up-quit this livin', pre-board that plane,
write an article or 2, upright the tray, admit the trap
and the but, enter the encyclopedia, visit
the museum of foreign arts, clothe myself
in a scruffy pink party dress and
black army boots and later
in black cutoff tights and a black shirt with an inspired sheen of re

slid along
every flat surface and railing in the performance space
of male stretch marks rubbing vitamin E crean
on what's left of the ethics
bath of pinkish light disappearing at times, then popping u
in another spot

i spent all the money i won after suing McDonald's for my morbid obesity
i hate homage so shut up
consummation alarm sirens as the bride is confused
by the broom nothing is amiss
teens loitering at the 7-11
or hanging out at the convenience store
could this have been me? elusive young potential
of biological and stem cell unimpeachable mess of jeans
svelte disheveled front suit me up to a mackerel supper
sleek skinned oily mackerel all laid-up on a bed of grains
cooked in a pot, tossed

side arm, unduly, lavishly, improvidently, into a barley field

delight and eat, eat and delete
the biftec, tender mushrooms the biotech the
buttons on a male collar,
sometimes the thought of how my world is made
gets me down, makes me blue
sometimes i wonder if there's anything to do
but to up-quit this livin', pre-board that plane,
open up a laundry, navigate the stain

drowning in
a teaspoon of water
"a person can drown in a teaspoon of water," said Deborah Cohen,
a life guard
it
doesn't take much to turn a sunny summer day and the logic of a hole
into a tragedy

last July at a Worcester pond,
Dorchester Street reservoir, Lake Cochituate, somebody dropped
a teaspoon on the beach and a toddler drowned said
a lakefront birthday party in Claresholm, she spits directly at the drain and
watches the aqua foam wind down the pipe, and starts to wash her hair, thinking about
how people can drown in a teaspoon of water, it reminds her that no matter how familiar
the routine, she is never really safe, and so she plugged all the sinks and shut off
the pipes, but no one told her
about the chocolate milk

as Pastor Bill reminded the spectators at the baptism in the Aquatic
Center's Jacuzzi last week, god doesn't allow us to say "well, i've lived a good life" just
"i wish i wasn't born with a silver spoon in my mouth or at least
a slotted spoon" when science, ethics, classics, and morals clash in a waterspot

sometimes the thought of how my world is made
gets me down, makes me blue
sometimes i wonder if there's anything to do
but to up-quit this livin', pre-board that plane,
use a spoon to scratch out my name
just before i drown

and realize that i, too, am just a battery
hooked up to the Matrix, there is no spoon, at
this point how many structures violate you, the reader? a man named maurice
led me down to middle earth
specifically, creation theory
can't prove anything
about male nipples
rockets can't protect them
they hate cake they
are a poor blanket
they hate foul kinds of microwaveable foreign imports with
irreplaceable spare parts for filthy greedy Tim Hortons chefs
sexy yet deadly in chef suits and oven mitts
neither wheat nor bales in the field fill the space
between the customs agents marshmallow stuck to the dry nose
of a stuffed moose head

ask dead buddha
stinking up
the school board office
the ancient odo(u)r of hypothalami
aches to
make me
a memory
a dream of post musical
or port-side coital attention
inside a cracked
crystal
ear
eating-hair for the consequences of

avoidance werewolf nuns and identical twins luckless
and inhuman
vulnerable napes lost clutch one other in fear and relief,
arrest over
and over one
other

you at the idolatry factory of we naked pressure ice down
the pants

sometimes the thought of how my world is made
gets me down, makes me blue
sometimes i wonder if there's anything to do
but to up-quit this livin', pre-board that plane,
puncture a nipple,
become a sensitive male through the pain

(dear canadian literature:
i fail to appear in your ranks as the
model appears in grey charcoal suit
but the food is good
and he gets laid.

return to the surface! the god in general said
but i couldn't hear or didn't listen
because

i had my head in the god of Anger's Armpit

heaven isn't on my side
and not even
up in the sky anywhere
so what are you trying to
point out the sky empty
of air Canada

never cum in a rented car.

having
a lunch

a coffee

a tea

is not like having

a chocolate bar

dear canada,

the leaning tower of Pisa isn't lazy,

just

bent

one of these things just doesn't belong. typical:

not the beef
but the hamburger
not the disease
but the trade embargo
not the lack of attention to the news
but the news' lack of attention to the me
for 40 days
and 40 nights
resist arrest the remote control and references
to the CBC and the NBC while in line

at the NY airport wondering
why not just apply for citizenship anyway

sometimes the thought of how my world is made
gets me down, makes me blue
sometimes i wonder if there's anything to do
but to up-quit this livin', pre-board that plane,
take up some industry, cultivate some ill-feelin's towards
the churches on main
how do they
get those human brains into such narrow-necked jars?

and
why put the whole brain in since you only use 10-20% of the damned thing anyway

fear of apprenticeships as
pop artisans taste of silk, apparent
smile
celestial musician carvings from a funeral couch ceaselessly
same faces wave from car windows eleven panels and two gate towers with relief
girl
standing woman with dog   carrying a leopard on her back
niche lintel rubbing shut store blocked ramp spring haze
court lady globular censor a set of two dancers and ten
entertainers   "let me compare thee to a summer's day"
let me elevate the panels and get relief for real! like

a moon
waxes and wanes
waxes and rebuffs
and re-waxes, loathes to lose the love pocked fetish of knees   it was
fetish of fetish cheese   her hand in my pants
and the sound of the ants; warm

this dirty cage with the sad voice that is no voice whe
upon the house slowly steps to mount
by no means almost white the world
riding through space tweaks with the boot piece
diminutive against this of pitiful bowing cockatoo
open door profits
mean the stars dear canada,

because my tears we have no such customs
fuel the eyes we have a car for every region manufactured
by nissan for every province
and one for the prairie poets too, and the
royal bank, several banks that are royal under a sky of dark boats fill the harb
with gin hanging scroll ink on paper

collection of the National Palace Museu
a place with a ball field, an alma matt
there is a god, there are two gods, there
a god for me and a god of impartial universality presiding ov
the perpetual pendulums epidemically unsuitable unive
free of newton's la

JULIA WILLIAMS

excerpt from *My Family Is a Genius*

after radiation Grandma went homeopathic, root vegetables, it doesn't take a genius. rumour of a woman who tried to cure her cancer with carrot juice but instead turned orange, went blind. Grandma read the Time Life series about the body and by the time she knew what her organs did they'd stopped.

Grandma wrote poetry when Amanda was born and Mum was embarrassed. you don't talk about poetry at home, you don't pretend your feelings are art. you don't ask for things, and you don't brag.

Grandma's poems in a box in the basement. poems for Amanda, rough drafts, sloped caps, notepaper edged in gingham. chickenscratch on the backs of cheques. prairie day trips, the strip of pavement that links Calgary and Carseland. "snow is light." pastoral.

this is a story of appeasement
bloody mindedness, bodies
insensate with genius

the most worthwhile part
its rampant dishonesty
simplicity. base misdirection.

“snow is height,” her lines short, syllable count marked in the margin. painstaking scansion: “snow is mine.” poetic feet. snow tracked down the left side of the page.

a poet is born from the most base ingredients and propped against human flesh.
touch her. she sings.

RITA WONG

fester

fester

fettered

fetid

fervid trade

traitor

ferocious trade

trap

fuel

fink trade feud

f k t e

gravytrainhasleftthestation

sweatshoparoundyourthroat

has the parody of a greed economy discounted your mother today?

value chain

how does one go about turning english from a low context language into a high context language?

tomorrow and tomorrow and tomorrow takes me back hundreds of years

the internal frontier: my consumer patterns

what is the context for "you people are hard workers?"

the electromagnetic fields of the refrigerator hum bewildered static *

cartons of cigarettes waiting for lungs to reside in

heaps of dolls burning for the sins of their owners

sometimes i open my mouth and my mother's words come tumbling out of me: don't go to sleep with wet hair or you'll get headaches when you're old

"they take your culture away from you: you cannot sing your own songs any-more"—overheard in a restaurant

utter english, the terrain has altered & *tong wa* won't "fit" into the compartment allotted for it

so much depends on a thin wok

the number of greens you can eat is limited only by your fear of pesticides. hello silent spring

the quick horizontal is better than a cup of caffeine most days

the military industrial complex is embedded in my imported electronics

* "Some scientists estimate that you are now daily exposed to 100 million times the EMF radiation of your grandparents." (http://www.clarus.com/aboutemf.html)

SUZANNE ZELAZO

Cataract

the first is a letter meant for compromise
sharp-edged
the shape of a man
lewd sediments
an advocation

under mystic scythe
the impact hesitates

fumbling over our own lassitude

odious
undoing it confuses the coupling

though less defiled by printing
the distortion adumbrates

Infusoria

a cameo
concentric recovering
we swallow the melody

moon signal achieves the tonnage
pale primeval goal of electric ecstasy
in memory and urns

unpeople the moment Claire
it's a topical underpass

mondial, it implies communion

the widening gyre
luminates

kaleidoscopic love affair

crescendo

mount the perspective
its light returns

influx mid-movement
cerebral calm
it's not the least echo
only the wreckage

the stasis is a flicker

elusive
save for the locution

it misses its own clarity

harmonic concordance
from Downsview to Danforth
in humming

sequential
moving through matter with your eyes closed

a redpath distillation

lakeview's plenty for the making

your braying's
sentient
the mirror cannot hold us both
though
together we sidle the exit

Vaga Luna

There is so much more than the language chosen to say it in. Soon there is a history between us, an amplification of the fact that we exist, mysterious. Each one another looking everywhere. The scars on all the beautiful women mark the lines I recite and over-write. Let us remake the world from the echo of our embrace, the sound of two bodies: electric. This pale trajectory of tomorrow, in all the moments of your unfolding. Above, the moon unravels before us, opens its soft wings to absence: a kiss, and the clouds settle, the way our clothes fall. Elliptical, the pause and continuum of sensation. Air damp on our skin, insistent flutter. Insomnia. Play me the round sound of union. Vertigo in remaking our transition into calm lucidity. Blue light vibrates, winged for the moment, our ways of filling space.

RACHEL ZOLF

excerpt from *Human Resources*

New performance weightings a bit of a moving target the future liability of make this sing.

Just to make sure we're speaking the same language we no longer have to use this caveat existing amounts grandfathered.

We'll have to wrap our heads around clear as mud I would like to move the goal posts.

Chunk it down into various links I'm totally medicated as I type.

A true copy of a copy, you defend the Sophists, use rhyme and pun in your heds and give me your best gut instinct. It's not as if the Republic sans poet pride in belgium part visual arsehole irene would repeat without knowing any less often than our 21st century Western simulacrum rife with scribbling nama zappa gerontology tricksters. Nor was Socrates' dialectical method for eliciting "truth" any less wily or rhetorical than drilling down through my inbox queued up for deterritorialized release, performance management

I don't want to trip over this in the future from where I'm sitting can you suggest massages.

This will give you a sense of the "new look" it seems the tail's wagging the tail this block of content has been rationalized.

This means we have to pass the punctum as sacred surplus I'll flip it over to you.

Forget the self without your pain you're nothing.

CONTRIBUTOR BIOS

derek beaulieu has been a past editor at both *filling Station* and *dANDelion* and a special editor of issues of *Whitewall of Sound* and *Open Letter*. In addition to his magazine editing work, he was also editor/publisher of housepress (1997-2004) and is the author of several books of poetry (*with wax*, Coach House Books, 2003; *frogments from the frag pool: haiku after Basho*, Mercury, 2005, with Gary Barwin). His poetry and artwork have appeared extensively in magazines and galleries across Canada. He has performed his work and discussed poetics and community across Canada, the UK, and the US. He lives in Calgary, with his young daughter, where he is administrative director at The New Gallery, an artist-run centre.

Gregory Betts is a Hamilton-based writer, born in Vancouver with Maritime roots. He has edited a few books, published in journals extensively, and recently published *If Language* (BookThug, 2005), his first book of poetry: an experimental exploration of the possibilities of the anagram. *If Language* was short-listed for the FitzPatrick O'Dinn Award (Rhode Island).

Alice Burdick is a poet living near Lunenburg in Nova Scotia. Her publications go back to the early 1990s, appearing through the grace of the Canadian small press, including Proper Tales Press, BookThug, Letters, and The Eternal Network. Her first spiny book is *Simple Master* (Pedlar Press, 2002); and poems have recently appeared in the magazines *fhole* and *Kinetic*, and in *Surreal Estate: 13 Canadian poets under the influence* (Mercury, 2004).

Jason Christie is a poet and visual artist who has lived in Milton, Toronto, and Calgary. In 2001, Jason graduated from York University's Creative Writing program. During his stay at York, he was an active member of the student collective Writers at York. In 2005, Jason completed his MA at the University of Calgary. Jason has been an editorial board member for *dANDelion*, *existere*, and *filling Station*. He was also the co-editor of *Open Letter*'s small press issue. Jason's popular community reading series, Yard, also spawned his micropress project, yardpress. Jason's first book of poetry, *Canada Post*, will be published by Snare Books in 2006. He recently compiled a collection of noise poems and plans to exhibit his visual poetry in the near future.

Michael deBeyer is the author of two books of poetry, *Rural Night Catalogue* (2002) and *Change in a Razor-backed Season* (2005), both published by Gaspereau Press. He received his MA in English from the University of New Brunswick. He currently lives and works in Fredericton.

Chris Fickling is a recent import to Manitoba. STOP. He spends his days as a minister, and nights as a doodler. STOP.

Jon Paul Fiorentino is the author of *Asthmatica* (a collection of comedic fiction) and *Hello Serotonin* (a collection of pharmaceutical poetry). He lives in Montréal where he is the managing editor of *Matrix*.

ryan fitzpatrick lives in Ogden, Calgary, Alberta and is poetry editor of *filling Station*. Coming from his newly finished manuscript *FAKE MATH*, the poems here attempt to channel the schizophrenic flows of information that engulf us daily as participants in high capitalist life. Composed primarily through the use of the Google internet search engine as a text generation device, these poems act as sieves, collecting and arranging relevant and intriguing cultural information for future contemplation and inquiry. Find more at his blog: http://process-documents.blogspot.com.

Jay Gamble lives in Calgary with his partner, Carmen, and their new baby boy, Lochlan. A PhD candidate at the University of Calgary, Jay is completing his dissertation on the Negative in Canadian Prairie Literature. The poems in this anthology are excerpted from a manuscript called *The Book of Knots*, which, ultimately, seeks to write not. He is obsessed with nothing.

Sharon Harris is a poet and artist whose column, "Fun with 'Pataphysics," has been a regular feature in *Word: Canada's Magazine for Readers + Writers* since January 2004. Her poems and photos have appeared in *jacket*, *Queen Street Quarterly*, *Rampike*, *broken pencil*, and won second place in *dANDelion*'s 2005 sci-fi contest. She has just finished a book-length manuscript of poems and is working on *I Love You*, a cultural study of those three little words. Her online home is http://iloveyougalleries.com.

Calgary born-and-bred poet Jill Hartman writes disjunctive narrative poetry about pachyderms, pirates, belly dancing, Ouija, Scrabble, and The Greatest Outdoor Show on Earth. Though her writing's been runner-up in the *Queen Street Quarterly* poetry contest and her first book of poetry, *A Painted Elephant* (Coach House Books, 2003), was short-listed for both the Stephansson and Lampert Awards, she has never actually been a bridesmaid (and will never be a bride).

Jamie Hilder is a Vancouver-based artist, critic, student, and labourer. His large scale wall drawing, *Paths and Places*, 2003, which documents his movements through urban and suburban environments over a period of one year, was recently exhibited at the Artspeak Gallery in Vancouver, and is represented in *Banlieusard*, an Artspeak publication. He is a PhD candidate in the English department at the University of British Columbia, and is currently training to run a mile in four minutes.

Geoffrey Hlibchuk is currently a PhD candidate at the State University of New York at Buffalo, where he is writing his dissertation on Canadian avant-garde writing. He is also the assistant director and webmaster of the North American Centre for Interdisciplinary Poetics.

Matthew Hollett is a poet and visual artist. His poetry has previously appeared in *Humber Mouths: New Voices from the West Coast of Newfoundland & Labrador*, and *The Backyards of Heaven: An Anthology of Contemporary Poetry from Ireland and Newfoundland & Labrador*. Matthew currently resides in Montréal, and maintains a website of artwork and writing at http://matthewhollett.com.

Jesse Huisken was born in 1980 in Toronto, where he continues to reside. He is a primarily self-taught artist and writer. His work as a visual artist has been conducted in traditional media: pencil, oil-paint, pen and ink. As a writer he has been the author of several smaller publications from Expert Press and BookThug. He is currently at work on an as yet untitled manuscript of extended verse works, and numerous smaller paintings.

Kedrick James' synaesthetic poetic brings oral, print, and digital arts into a public research-based practice. Cross-media/genre collaborations AWOL LOVE VIBE, VERBOMOTORHEAD, and http://pointlesshysteria.com have resulted in several publications and recordings; the book by AWOL, *Exstatic Almanac: a book of daze*, with CD, (Insomniac, 1997) is a personal favourite. Creator of poetry documentaries for CBC, BravoTV, more recently he has produced public experiments in State Induction and the use of Visionary Technologies for video release, and is working on a new book, titled *Curriculum of the Damned*.

Reg Johanson teaches composition and literature at Capilano College in North Vancouver, Coast Salish Territory. An ex-member of the Kootenay School of Writing Collective, his writing has appeared in KSW's *W4* and *W6*, *West Coast Line*, *The Rain Review of Books*, and *Companions & Horizons: An Anthology of Simon Fraser University Writers* (West Coast Line Writers, 2005). Work on Annharte is forthcoming in an anthology of criticism on radical women writers, and new poetry is forthcoming from Troyka Editions. He is a founding member of the Pacific Institute of Language and Literacy Studies.

Frances Kruk was born and raised in the heart of beef, Calgary, Alberta. She has been to university and now runs with scissors in one hand and pre-fabricated spitballs in the other. She is an interdisciplinary trickster squatting in the realm of audio-visual poetics and misinformation.

Larissa Lai is an animal/machine/human hybrid who has inadvertently stumbled out of a late-nineteenth-century time machine and found herself in the wrong millennium. Her geographic trajectory includes San Diego, Ames, St. John's, Hong Kong, Vancouver, Norwich, and Calgary but she still has several more rocket stages to jettison before her satellite goes into permanent orbit. She has written two novels: *When Fox Is a Thousand* and *Salt Fish Girl*; and a bunch of chapbooks: *Sybil Unrest* (with Rita Wong), *Rachel*, *Maria*, *Nascent Fashion*, and *Welcome to Asian Women in Business*. *West Coast Line* has recently published a special issue addressing her work.

Jason Le Heup is a member of The Prize Budget for Boys, creators of *The Spectacular Vernacular Revue* (Roof, 2004) and ARTAI Blue Chip Games™. He hosted Terrence Dish (Toronto, 2001), a daily reading of materials proposed by a large email list through a street-level apartment intercom. With Chris Walker, he produced the project *Judy* and with Mathew Riseborough he ran Karma Killed Elvis, a production company based in Vancouver. Jason currently manages an international outsourcing practice for one of the "Big 4" American professional services firms.

Glen Lowry lives and works in Vancouver, BC. He is a scholar, teacher, editor, writer, and photographer and his works, critical and creative, have appeared in a number of books and journals, including most recently *The Walrus* and *Mosaic*. His afterword was published with a new version of Roy Kiyooka's *Transcanada Letters* (NeWest, 2005). He is presently working on "After the End/s of CanLit," a scholarly manuscript focused on CanLit's recent past. Lowry co-edits *West Coast Line*, an SFU-based literary and cultural journal.

Danielle Maveal has a BA from York University's Creative Writing Program and a Diploma in Jewellery Arts from George Brown College. She sleeps in half a walnut shell and snowboards on a strawberry leaf. Danielle secretly stands up in Toronto and uses Stein's *Tender Buttons* as an umbreller. She is currently experimenting with the use of acrylic and precious materials to create wearable art.

Jeremy Mcleod lives and writes in Kingston, Ontario. He currently makes his living boarding and taping drywall. Sometimes his knuckles and hands hurt too much to type poetry.

Max Middle is a founding member of the music, sound, poetry, performance experiment known as the Max Middle Sound Project. The latter has staged five performances since their debut at the 2004 Ottawa Fringe Festival, including one in spring 2005 at the Ottawa International Writers Festival. More about him can be gleaned online at http://www.maxmiddle.com and an interview along with some poems appears in Ottawater at http://www.ottawater.com. In March 2005, above/ground press published a second chapbook authored by Max, this one titled *smthg*.

gustave morin, professional chainsaw juggler and maker of "a few poetry," is the "brains" behind the conspiracy known as S.P.A., and the author of some 4 books in and out of print, most recently, *a penny dreadful* (2003).

Janet Neigh subscribes to an unlimited long distance plan for calling anywhere in North America. "The Wiring of Bella O" is an excerpt from *Tele*, a work-in-progress. She has spent most of her life living in different parts of Canada. Currently, she lives in Philadelphia where she is working on a PhD in Literature at Temple University. Her writing can be found in *HOW2*, *West Coast Line*, and *filling Station*.

a.rawlings is a poet, editor, and multidisciplinary artist. Born in Indiana, raised in rural Northern Ontario, and a current resident of Toronto, she recently presented work in Alberta, Illinois, Newfoundland, New York, and Ontario. In 2001, Angela received the bpNichol Award for Distinction in Writing when she graduated from York University. Since then, she has worked with a variety of literary organizations, including The Mercury Press, The Scream Literary Festival, Sumach Press, *Word: Canada's Magazine for Readers + Writers*, and The Lexiconjury Reading Series. In 2005, Angela hosted the poetry documentary series *Heart of a Poet*. Angela's first book-length collection of poetry, *Wide slumber for lepidopterists* (Coach House Books), will be published in 2006. Angela also works in theatre and dance.

Rob Read grew up near Komoka, Ontario. He presently lives in Toronto where he writes and publishes through his small press, Produce Press. His published works include *See Rob Read, Read Rob Read* (Palimpsest Press, 2000), *Hieroglyphs* (The Expert Press, 2001), *Open Letter, Closed Book* (with AEM, Produce Press, 2004), and *Atone Neither Overflowing Clause* (with AEM, Produce Press, 2005). His first trade book *O Spam, Poams* (BookThug, 2005) features a selection of poems from his ongoing Daily Treated Spams. For more information or to sign up to receive Daily Treated Spam, please visit http://www.dailytreatedspam.com, or email readrobread@hotmail.com.

Jordan Scott's first book of poetry, *Silt*, was published by New Star Books in 2005. His second manuscript, *blert*, which explores the poetics of the stutter, is still searching for a home. Jordan likes manatees, stoops, and Calgary mornings.

Natalie Simpson is a former *filling Station* managing editor whose poems have appeared in *West Coast Line*, *Queen Street Quarterly*, and *dANDelion*. She has also published chapbooks through housepress and MODL Press. More poems are forthcoming in the anthology *Post-Prairie* from Talonbooks. She is currently finishing a manuscript about working in the oil and gas industry in Calgary, and she may one day write about studying law in Vancouver.

Trevor Speller is currently studying English Literature at the State University of New York at Buffalo. His poetry appears intermittently in small Canadian magazines and is often self-published. Currently on creative hiatus, significant work will appear in 2006.

Nathalie Stephens writes in English and French, and sometimes neither. Writing l'entre-genre, she is the author of several published works, most recently *L'Injure* (l'Hexagone, 2004), *Paper City* (Coach House Books, 2003), *Je Nathanaël* (l'Hexagone, 2003), and *Somewhere Running* (Arsenal Pulp, 2000). *L'Injure* was a finalist for the 2005 Prix Trillium; *Underground* (TROIS, 1999) was short-listed in 2000 for the Grand Prix du Salon du livre de Toronto. Stephens has presented her work internationally, notably in Barcelona, Chicago, Norwich, Ljubljana, Iowa City, and New York. She is the recipient of a 2002 Chalmers Arts Fellowship and a 2003 British Centre for Literary Translation Residential Bursary. She has translated Catherine Mavrikakis and François Turcot into English and Gail Scott and R. M. Vaughan into French. On occasion, she translates herself. She lives between.

Andrea Strudensky lives and works in Buffalo, New York. She has high hopes.

Hugh Thomas teaches mathematics at the University of New Brunswick. A chapbook of his poetry, *Mutations*, was published in 2004 by BookThug. The poem "Welcome" was begun while poet-in-residence at Motel Nooitgedacht. Thanks to Karen Mac Cormack, Jay MillAr, Stuart Ross, and Jason Taniguchi for their help and encouragement.

Mark Truscott's first book, *Said Like Reeds or Things* (Coach House Books, 2004), was short-listed for a ReLit award and received an Alcuin citation for Darren Wershler-Henry's design. Mark lives in Toronto, where he co-edits the magazine *BafterC* and runs the Test Reading Series.

douglas webster was born in Kitchener-Waterloo and spent his early years in Midland Bay Woods, Ontario. He's got a BA in Creative Writing from York University, and currently resides in Toronto.

Jonathon Wilcke is a musician and poet living in Vancouver. His first book, *Pornograph*, was released by Red Deer Press in 2004. His writing also appears in *Fiddlehead*, *filling Station*, *dANDelion*, *Open Letter*, and *The Capilano Review*. He is a member of the Kootenay School of Writing Collective.

Julia Williams is a freelance writer whose poetry has appeared in *The Literary Review of Canada*, *Queen Street Quarterly*, *filling Station*, *CV2*, and *This Magazine*. Her first book, *The Sink House*, was published by Coach House Books in 2004. Despite having had good fortune as a poet, Julia aspires to be a novelist. She lives in Calgary with her husband and her stuff.

rita wong's book of poems, *monkeypuzzle*, was published by Press Gang in 1998, for which she received the Asian Canadian Writers' Workshop Emerging Writer Award. She is an assistant professor in critical & cultural studies at the Emily Carr Institute in Vancouver. She is working on a second book, tentatively entitled *present imperfect*.

Suzanne Zelazo is a PhD candidate in English at York University, the author of *Parlance* (Coach House Books, 2003), and the editor of and publisher of *Queen Street Quarterly*.

Toronto poet Rachel Zolf's practice is situated near the limits of language and the page. She creates polyvocal assemblages from found fragments, long poems that work by accretion with montage shock effects. Themes that include subjectivity, cultural identity, sexuality and trauma stew in wry anti-aesthetic language/lyric explorations of the modern familiar. This selection of poems comes from her work-in-progress, *Human Resources*, a book that is a kind of writing machine, wasting words and generating words as waste. Zolf's second book, *Masque* (Mercury, 2004), was nominated for the 2005 Trillium Book Award for Poetry. She serves as poetry editor for *The Walrus* magazine.

ACKNOWLEDGEMENTS

DEREK BEAULIEU: "variance" appeared online through greenboathouse books; "for Brian" originally appeared as a housepress leaflet; "pitt graphit 4" appeared as part of *[the orange manifesto]* (MODL Press, 2005).

GREGORY BETTS: The love poem previously appeared in *Love*, a chapbook. Anagrams excerpted from *If Language* (BookThug, 2005).

MICHAEL DEBEYER: "Penultimate Iceworks" appeared in *Lichen Literary Journal*; "The Party" appeared in *The Antigonish Review*; "The Frictionless Room" appeared in *Queen's Quarterly*; "Light as Air" (earlier version) appeared in *Harpweaver*; all poems excerpted from *Change in a Razor-backed Season* (Gaspereau Press, 2005).

JON PAUL FIORENTINO: All poems excerpted from *The Theory of the Loser Class* (Coach House Books, 2006).

SHARON HARRIS: "Fun with 'Pataphysics" previously appeared in *Word: Canada's Magazine for Readers + Writers* and the chapbook *Fun with 'Pataphysics* (BookThug, 2005). The collage was published in *Queen Street Quarterly* and was part of "Eye Scream: A Night of Visual Poetry" at Virus Arts Gallery and Objectorium. All of her work is part of a work-in-progress manuscript, *AVATAR*.

JILL HARTMAN: Parts of *Another Word for Pirate Treasure, or, The Booty* have been published in the chapbook *Pirate Lore* (MODL Press, 2005), as *Ménage a Trois* (DIAGRAM 5.1), in *filling Station* issue 30, in *A dANDy Chappie* (dANDelion Chapbooks, 2004), as a chapbook titled *Another Word for Pirate Treasure, or, The Booty* (housepress, 2003), part of the broadside anthology *Shelf* (housepress, 2003), and in *YARD* issue 2.

MATTHEW HOLLETT: All poems have previously appeared on http://matthewhollett.com. "rabbit-track alphabet" is from *alphabetica* and "speechballoon #0217" is a still from an interactive Flash project called *speechballoon*.

MAX MIDDLE: "dear jc" was published as an above/ground press broadside #207 in 2004; "Visual Poem 1" published May 2005 untitled in *Murderous Signs*, Issue 11; "Visual Poem 2" published March 2005 untitled in *smthg*, an above/ground press chapbook.

GUSTAVE MORIN: "ACK" first published in N.A.C.'s *Arts and Literary* #2 (winter 2004); "index" first published in *The Berkeley Horse*, #48 (1993), later collected in *p.mody's dada boutique* (1997);"derail" from *Sun Kissed Oranges* (1995); "voice" from *A Penny Dreadful* (2003); "going nova" first appeared in *VAN* (2000).

A.RAWLINGS: "Narcolepsy," "Somniloquy," and "love poem for a sailor" excerpted from *Wide slumber for lepidopterists* (Coach House Books, 2006). Versions of "Somniloquy" have previously appeared in *filling Station* and *West Coast Line.*

NATALIE SIMPSON: A version of "TIDE" appeared in *sudden magazine 1340*, and a version of "Vallarta" appeared in *endNote* 3/4.

TREVOR SPELLER: "famous people./" appeared in a private chapbook entitled *the launch point*, self-published in December 2002; "Magnolia acuminata" appeared as part of housepress' shelf broadside series.

HUGH THOMAS: All poems previously appeared in *Mutations* (BookThug, 2004).

MARK TRUSCOTT: All poems previously appeared in *Said Like Reeds or Things* (Coach House Books, 2004).

THANK YOU

The editors wish to thank BookThug, Coach House Books, and Gaspereau Press for the generous permission to reprint texts; and above/ground, dANDelion chapbooks, housepress, and MODL for publishing these texts through smallpress editions. Thank you to Beverley Daurio, Nate Dorward, Chris Ewart, Jon Paul Fiorentino, Conor Green, Benedict Hynes, Sandy Lam, Jay MillAr, Katherine Parrish, Andrea Ryer, Jordan Scott, and the contributors for their support and encouragement. Brendan Fernandes' support through his kind permission to use his cover artwork also was greatly appreciated.